BRANCH LINES AROUND

AVONMOUTH

Hotwells, Severn Beach
and via Henbury

Vic Mitchell and Keith Smith

MP Middleton Press

Cover picture: The oldest part of Bristol Temple Meads is in the background of this atmospheric record from 1956. It is now walled off to house an exhibition hall as part of the British and Commonwealth Museum. A wider view and more details can be found in picture 3. (P.J.Kelley)

ACKNOWLEDGEMENTS

We are very grateful for the assistance received from many of those mentioned in the credits also to A.E.Bennett, W.R.Burton, L.Crosier, G.Croughton, N.Langridge, D.T.Rowe, Mr D. and Dr S.Salter, M.Tozer, E.Wilmshurst and particularly our always supportive wives, Barbara Mitchell and Janet Smith.

Published September 2004

ISBN 1 904474 42 X

© Middleton Press, 2004

Design   Deborah Esher
David Pede

Published by
Middleton Press
Easebourne Lane
Midhurst, West Sussex
GU29 9AZ
Tel: 01730 813169
Fax: 01730 812601
Email: info@middletonpress.co.uk
www.middletonpress.co.uk

Printed & bound by Biddles Ltd, Kings Lynn

CONTENTS

INDEX

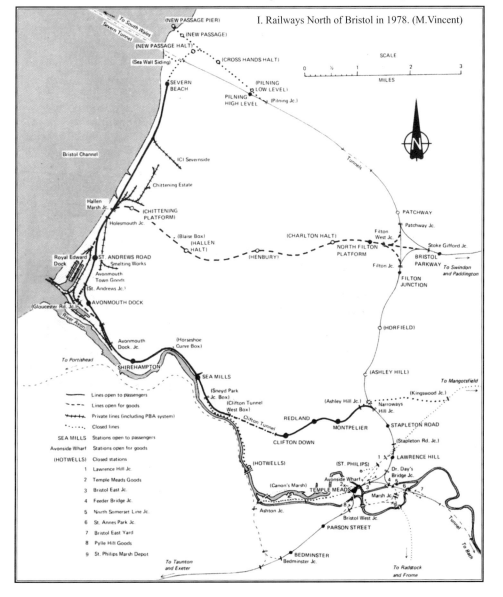

I. Railways North of Bristol in 1978. (M. Vincent)

GEOGRAPHICAL SETTING

With an inland port, the ancient trading centre of Bristol had prospered and its status was enhanced with the creation of a non-tidal harbour in 1804-09. The city is sheltered on its western flank by a high ridge of Limestone, which rises to over 250ft at Clifton Down and is cut through by the Avon Gorge. This is spanned by the famous Clifton Suspension Bridge, but the Avon's meandering course made access to the urban port difficult. This fact, combined with the increasing size of ships, resulted in the building of a dock at Avonmouth, which was opened in 1877.

The level clays in this area were ideal for other commercial development, particularly industries requiring marine transport. The high ground north of Bristol attracted the aircraft industry, as its fairly level nature was suitable for an east-west runway.

This upland area resulted in severe gradients on the railway north from Bristol and the three lines eastwards were built partly in tunnel. The tiny River Trym has had little impact on the railways of the district.

The maps are to the scale of 25ins to 1 mile, with north at the top, unless otherwise indicated.

HISTORICAL BACKGROUND

The Great Western Railway's first line in the area was between Bath and Bristol Temple Meads and it came into use on 31st August 1840. The Bristol & Gloucester Railway and the Bristol & Exeter Railway were both completed in the Bristol area in the early 1840s. The BGR became part of the Midland Railway in 1846 and the BER was a section of the GWR main line from 1876.

The Bristol & South Wales Union Railway opened a broad gauge single line northwards from Bristol to its pier on the River Severn at New Passage on 8th September 1863. It became part of the GWR on 1st August 1868 and was converted to standard gauge on 7-9th August 1873.

The Bristol Port Railway & Pier Company opened a line between Avonmouth and Hotwells on 6th March 1865, the latter terminus being situated under the east end of the Clifton Suspension Bridge. The line was not connected to any other until a joint GWR/MR initiative created the Clifton Extension Railway. This allowed MR trains from Fishponds and GWR services from Temple Meads to reach Clifton Down from 1st October 1874. The section west thereof to the BPR&P line carried freight from 24th February 1877 and passengers from 1st September 1885. The line to Avonmouth became a joint operation and was bought by the GWR and MR in 1890.

The Severn Tunnel opened for passenger services on 1st December 1886, trains using most of the New Passage line. This was doubled in 1887 and the part west of Pilning became a siding.

The next major development in the area was the completion of a direct line between Swindon and the tunnel (The South Wales & Bristol Direct) in 1903. An earlier initiative had been the completion of a single goods line between Pilning and Avonmouth on 5th February 1900. This carried passengers from 9th July 1928. (The part south of Severn Beach had opened to passengers on 5th June 1922.) The final link was formed by the Avonmouth & Filton Railway on 9th May 1910. This gave a direct route between the 1903 main line and Avonmouth Docks via Henbury; it conveyed passengers from the outset. All these lines were part of the GWR.

Upon nationalisation in 1948, the GWR became the Western Region of British Railways. Passenger withdrawals took place thus: Fishponds to Montpelier on 31st March 1941, Severn Beach to Pilning on 23rd November 1964 and Avonmouth to Filton on 5th July 1965. The short length to Hotwells had closed completely on 19th September 1921, although Hotwells Halt was in use until 30th July 1922.

Privatisation gave Prism Rail a franchise for Wales & West for 7½ years from 13th October 1996, later extended to March 2006. The name was changed to Wessex Trains in 2001, for local trains in this area.

PASSENGER SERVICES

Down trains only are considered in this section.

Bristol & South Wales Union Railway

Six trains on weekdays and three on Sundays appeared in the 1869 timetable. Often a note stated that ferries connected with trains. The reverse was often the case, owing to the ferries being delayed by the tide or the weather.

In many cases, Pilning had only one train call each day, but by 1884 there were three. There were then eight to the ferry on weekdays and two on Sundays. The tunnel construction workers had increased traffic on the line.

To Avonmouth

The first timetable showed eight trains from Hotwells (then named Clifton), this increasing to nine by 1869, when there were six on Sundays. The figures were ten and two in 1911, but had declined to eight and none prior to the Hotwells section of that route closing in 1922.

In the meantime, the frequency increased with through running via Clifton Down in 1885. Six from there were added to the ten from Hotwells on weekdays.

Eighteen from Temple Meads and ten from Hotwells were on offer on weekdays by 1911. The total in 1928 was 20 on weekdays and 5 on Sundays. Few changes followed, the figures being 18 and 2 in 1964 with 15 and 0 in 1984. A similar service has been operated to Severn Beach subsequently, except during the last two weeks of June 2004, when it was suspended to allow long distance trains to run non-stop via Avonmouth during the rebuilding of Filton Abbey Wood.

To Clifton Down

The initial service comprised 13 weekday trains with five on Sundays. By 1876, some trains were originating at Weston-super-Mare. Most GWR trains started at Temple Meads, while the MR ones came from St. Philips, which was more convenient to the city centre.

Clifton Down was receiving 37 trains from Bristol by 1910, 20 of which terminated there. By 1929 only three terminated and a decade later there were none. Thus the Avonmouth service applied thereon.

North to Severn Beach

Trains ran for holidaymakers from June to October 1922 and from April to October 1923. It was to be May 1924 before a regular all-year service began. The October 1923 timetable showed four trains, weekdays only, while the one for July 1924 contained twelve, with three on Sundays.

Severn Beach to Pilning

A generous service of nine weekday and four Sunday trains was provided initially. Seven trains were operated for much of the 1930s-40s, but Sunday services were curtailed during WWII. The number was down to five or six from the mid-1950s to the end. By this period, many of the trains operated only between Severn Beach and Pilning Low Level, instead of a circular route.

Fishponds to Clifton Down

The frequency diminished from 13 to 8 on weekdays and from 3 to 2 on Sundays. Trains ran from Bath, Mangotsfield or Fishponds until 1941.

Via Henbury

A weekdays-only service of seven trains ran from Temple Meads via Filton Junction to an exclusive GWR terminus known as "Avonmouth Docks", in use for the first five years. Six trains were the norm between the wars, but only four appeared during the final years. They mostly operated a circular service, out from and back to Temple Meads.

Timetable extracts

As the workings were complex, overlapping and sometimes stopped short, a large number of samples follow for detailed study. Some 1955 extracts can be found near picture 107.

Offices—Bristol.] BRISTOL and SOUTH WALES UNION.—Great Western. [Sec., L. Bruton.

Down.	Week Days.						Sundays.		
From London, p. 8. / ,, *Exeter, p.* 10.	1,2,3 clss	1&2 a	1&2 d	1&2 b	1,2,3 clss	1,2,3 clss	1,2,3 clss	1,2,3 clss	1,2,3 clss
Temple Mead Sta.,	mrn	mrn	aft	aft	aft	aft	mrn	aft	aft
Bristol ....dep	6 15	10 0	1215	3 0	5 0	6 [illegible]	8 10	3 0	7 20
Lawrence Hill........	6 20	10 5	1220	3 5	5 5	6 55	8 15	3 5	7 25
Stapleton Road	6 23	10 8	1223	3 10	5 8	6 58	8 18	3 10	7 28
Ashley Hill.........	6 27	1012	....	....	....	7 2	8 22	3 15	....
Filton	6 33	1018	....	....	....	7 8	8 28	3 23	....
Patchway..........	6 41	1025	1233	3 25	5 18	7 16	8 34	3 30	7 40
Pilning	6 50	....	....	....	....	7 25	8 42	3 40	....
New Passage	7 0	1040	1245	3 40	5 30	7 33	8 50	3 50	7 55
Portskewet J 28, 29	7 45	1130	1 20	4 20	6 15	8 15	9 20	4 40	8 25
Chepstow 29 arr	8 10	1150	1 35	5 15	6 35	8 25	9 45	5 6	....
Newport 28.. ,,	8 30	1155	1 52	5 20	6 47	8 40	10 8	5 20	9 0
Cardiff 28 .. ,,	8 55	1220	2 20	5 55	7 10	9 5	1036	5 47	9 30

d Passengers booked through to Waterford.

Up.	Wk Days			Sundays.				
	mrn	mrn	aft	mrn	aft	aft	aft	aft
Cardiff 29 ..dep	7 35	9 35	1231	8 15	3 56	2 40	4 5	....
Newport 29.... ,,	8 0	10 0	1 30	8 40	4 23	3 5	4 30	....
Chepstow 28 .. ,,	8 15	10 5	1 17	9 18	4 38	....	4 40	8 5
From South Wales Line, see pp. 28 & 29.	1,2,3	1&2	1&2	1,2,3	1,2,3	1,2,3	1,2,3	1,2,3
	mrn	c	aft	mrn	aft	aft	aft	aft
Portskewet Junc. d	8 30	1025	2 20	9 30	5 0	3 30	5 5	8 20
New Passage	9 5	11 0	3 10	10 5	5 40	4 0	5 45	4 0
Pilning	9 10	....	....	1011	....	....	....	....
Patchway	9 20	1112	3 25	1021	5 55	4 15	5 57	9 15
Filton	9 28	....	....	1027	....	4 21	....	9 21
Ashley Hill.........	9 32	....	3 35	1033	6 5	4 27	....	9 27
Stapleton Road	9 38	1122	3 38	1036	6 10	4 30	6 10	9 30
Lawrence Hill........	....	1127	3 41	1039	6 13	4 33	6 15	9 33
Bristol 9, 10, 170 a	9 45	1135	3 50	1045	6 25	4 50	6 22	9 40

a Pass. not booked East of Chepstow. b 3rd cl. to Great Western Stas. East & West of Portskewet. c 3rd cl. from all Great Western Stations West of Portskewet. ☞ Steam Boats ply across the Passage to meet Trains on either side.

Gen. Man., Charles Wilkinson.] BRISTOL PORT and PIER. [Sec., Hew Dalrymple.

Miles.	Fares. 1 cl. s. d.	2 cl. s. d.	3 cl. s. d.	Return. 1 cl s. d.	2 cl s. d.	Down.	Week Days. gov	aft	aft	aft	aft	aft	aft	aft	aft		Sundays. gov	aft	aft	aft	aft	aft	
						Clifton........dep	9 30	1230	2 30	3 30	4 30	5 30	6 30	7 30	9 30	....	3 0	4 0	5 30	6 30	8 0	9 30	....
2	0 6	0 4	0 3	0 9	0 6	Sea Mills	9 40	1240	2 40	3 40	4 40	5 40	6 40	7 40	9 40	....	3 10	4 10	5 40	6 40	8 10	9 40	....
3½	0 10	0 7	0 4	1 3	0 11	Shirehampton	9 48	1248	2 48	3 48	4 48	5 48	6 48	7 48	9 48	....	3 18	4 18	5 48	6 48	8 18	9 48	....
5½	1 0	0 9	0 6	1 6	1 3	Avonmouth ...arr	9 55	1255	2 55	3 55	4 55	5 55	6 55	7 55	9 55	....	3 25	4 25	5 55	6 55	8 25	....	....

Mls	Fares. 1 cl.	2 cl.	3 cl.	Return. 1 cl.	2 cl.	Up.	gov	noon	aft	aft	aft	aft	aft	aft	aft	aft	gov	aft	aft	aft	aft	aft	
						Avonmouth ..dep	9 0	12 0	2 0	3 0	4 0	5 0	6 0	7 0	9 0	10 0	2 30	3 30	5 0	6 0	7 30	9 0	....
2½	0 9	0 6	0 3	1 2	0 9	Shirehampton	9 7	12 7	2 7	3 7	4 7	5 7	6 7	7 7	9 7	10 7	2 37	3 37	5 7	6 7	7 37	9 7	....
3½	0 11	0 8	0 5	1 5	1 [illegible]	Sea Mills	9 15	1215	2 15	3 15	4 15	5 15	6 15	7 15	9 15	....	2 45	3 45	5 15	6 15	7 45	9 15	....
5½	1 0	0 9	0 6	1 6	1 3	Clifton ....arr	9 25	1225	2 25	3 25	4 25	5 25	6 25	7 25	9 25	1025	2 55	3 55	5 25	6 25	7 55	9 25	....

June 1869

BATH, BRISTOL, and CLIFTON DOWN.—Midland.

Mls	Fares 1 cl.	3 cl.	Midland Station,	mrn	mrn	a	mrn	a	mrn	a	aft	a	aft	aft	a	a	aft	aft	aft	Sundays. a	aft	aft
—			Bath............dep	....	7 25	8 35	9 55	1040	1135	1 10	....	3 0	4 15	6 0	6 35	7 15	....	9 0	10 5	8 40	1 30	6 40
¾	0 3	0 1	Weston	....	7 28	8 38	9 58	1043	....	1 13	....	3 3	4 18	....	6 38	7 18	....	9 3	10 8	8 43	1 33	6 43
4	0 7	0 4	Kelston, for Saltford	....	....	8 46	....	1051	....	1 21	....	....	4 26	....	6 46	7 26	....	9 11	....	8 51	1 37	6 51
6¼	0 11	0 6	Bitton.............	....	7 38	8 52	10 8	1057	....	1 27	....	3 14	4 32	6 12	6 52	7 32	....	9 17	1018	8 57	1 41	6 57
8½	1 3	0 8½	Warmley	....	7 43	8 57	1013	11 2	....	1 32	....	3 19	4 37	....	6 57	7 37	....	9 22	1023	9 2	1 52	7 2
9¾	1 4	0 9½	Mangotsfield.. arr	....	7 47	9 1	1017	11 6	1150	1 36	....	3 23	4 41	....	7 1	7 41	....	9 26	1027	9 6	1 56	7 6
			Mangotsfield.. dep	....	7 49	9 4	1020	11 7	1152	1 40	....	3 28	4 43	....	7 6	7 42	7 51	9 28	1029	9 8	1 58	7 8
12¼	1 7	0 11½	Fish Ponds	5 30	7 56	9 11	1026	1113	1158	1 46	....	3 34	4 49	6 23	7 12	....	....	9 34	1036	9 14	2 4	7 14
—	....	....	Fish Ponds....dep	....	....	9 35	1032	1118	12 0	1 52	2 17	3 49	4 55	6 29	7 18	....	7 57	9 40	....	....	....	....
15¼	....	....	Montpellier	....	....	9 43	1040	1126	12 8	2 0	2 25	3 57	5 3	6 37	7 26	....	8 5	9 48	....	....	....	....
16½	....	....	Clifton Down arr	....	....	9 48	1045	1131	1213	2 5	2 30	4 2	5 8	6 42	7 31	....	8 10	9 53	....	....	....	....
—	2 0	0 11½	Bristol (Temple St.)	....	....	9 40	....	1135	....	2 10	....	3 50	....	....	7 45	8 0	....	....	....	1015	....	....
15¼	2 0	0 11½	,, St. Philip's 15	5 37	8 3	9 20	1035	1122	1210	1 55	....	3 43	4 58	6 32	7 21	....	....	9 43	1043	9 23	2 13	7 23

a Temple Street Passengers change at Mangotsfield.

June 1876

HOTWELLS, SEA MILLS, and AVONMOUTH DOCK (Joint).—G. W. and Mid.

Miles.	Down.	Week Days. mrn	mrn	mrn	mrn	aft	aft	aft	aft	aft	aft	Sundays. aft	aft
—	Hotwells ....dep.	6 20	7 5	8 45	11 0	1 0	2 40	4 32	5 55	7 10	9 0	2 45	8 40
2	Sea Mills...............	....	....	....	11 8	1 8	2 48	4 41	6 3	7 18	....	....	....
3½	Shirehampton	6 35	7 21	9 0	1115	1 15	2 55	4 48	6 10	7 25	9 15	3 1	8 56
5	Avonmouth Dock (Jnt)	6 40	7 25	9 4	1119	1 19	3 0	4 52	6 14	7 29	9 19	3 5	9 0

Mls	Joint Station.	mrn	mrn	mrn	mrn	aft	aft	aft	aft	aft	aft	aft	aft
—	Avonmouth Dock dep.	6 0	6 45	8 15	9 35	1233	2 10	4 5	5 25	6 30	8 30	2 20	8 15
1½	Shirehampton	6 5	6 50	8 20	9 40	1238	2 15	4 10	5 30	6 36	8 35	2 25	8 20
3	Sea Mills...............	....	....	....	9 46	1245	2 22	4 16	5 37	6 42	....	....	....
5	Hotwells ....arr.	6 16	7 1	8 33	9 53	1252	2 29	4 23	5 44	6 51	8 49	2 39	8 34

BRISTOL, FILTON JUNCTION, and AVONMOUTH DOCKS (**Motor Cars—One class only**).—G. W.

Miles.	Down. Temple Meads Station,	Week Days. mrn	mrn	mrn	aft	aft	Weds. only	aft	aft	aft	Sundays.
—	Bristol ....dep.	6a55	8g5	10a10	12a23	2a20		3a45	5a30	7 3	
1	Lawrence Hill	7 3	8g10	10 20	12 30	2 25		3 55	5 40	7 7	
1¾	Stapleton Road..........	7 7	8g15	10 23	12 33	2 30		3 58	5 44	7 10	
2½	Ashley Hill..............	7 11	8g20	10 26	12 36	2 34		4 1	5 48	7 13	
4¾	Filton Junction ¶	7 19	8 32	10 34	12 44	2 42		4 9	5 57	7 21	
7¾	Henbury ¶	7 28	8 41	10 43	12 53	2 51		4 18	6 6	7 30	
12¾	Avonmouth Dks (G. W.)	7 40	8 53	9 55	1 5	3 3		4 30	6 18	7 42	

Mls	Gt. Western Station,	mrn	mrn	mrn	aft	Weds. only	aft	aft	aft	aft
—	Avonmouth Dks ¶ dep.	8 5	9 25	11 0	1 40		3 15	4 50	6 30	8 50
5	Henbury ¶	8 17	9 37	1112	1 52		3 27	5 2	6 42	9 2
8	Filton Junction 60, 64..	8 27	9 47	1122	2 2		3 37	5 12	6 52	9 12
10¼	Ashley Hill	8g39	9 52	1127	2 7		3 42	5 17	6 57	9 17
11	Stapleton Road..........	8g42	9 57	1131	2 11		3 47	5 21	7 1	9 20
11½	Lawrence Hill	8g44	10 0	1133	2 13		3 49	5 23	7 3	9 22
12¼	Bristol (Temple M.) arr.	8g50	10a11	11[illegible]a	2 29		4a10	5a35	7 10	9 28

NOTES.

a Temple Meads Passengers change at Stapleton Road.
g Change at Filton Junction.
¶ "**Halts**" at Filton and Charlton, between Filton Junction and Henbury; and Hallen, between Henbury and Avonmouth Docks.

October 1911

October 1923

BRISTOL, CLIFTON DOWN, AVONMOUTH DOCK, and SEVERN BEACH.—G. W. and L. M. & S.

Miles	Down.	Week Days. mrn	mrn	mrn	mrn	mrn	mrn	mrn	mrn	mrn	mrn	mrn	mrn
—	Bristol (Temple Meads) dep.	5 10	....	....	....	7 10	7 17	8 2	8 37	9 20	10 0	1045	1125
1	Lawrence Hill	5 14	....	....	....	7 15	7 22	8 7	8 41	9 24	10 4	1049	1129
1½	Stapleton Road	5 17	6 14	....	....	7 18	7 25	8 10	8 44	9 27	10 7	1052	1132
2¼	Montpelier	5 21	6 19	....	....	7 24	7 30	8 15	8 48	9 31	1011	1056	1136
3¼	Redland	....	....	....	....	7 27	7 33	8 18	8 51	9 34	1014	1059	1139
4	Clifton Down ...... arr.	5 25	6 23	....	....	7 29	7 35	8 20	8 53	9 36	1016	11 1	1141
	Clifton Down ...... dep.	5 26	6 25	7 19	....	7 31	7 37	8 22	8 55	9 37	1018	11 2	1142
6	Sea Mills	....	6 31	7 25	....	....	7 43	8 28	9 0	9 42	1023	11 7	1147
7½	Shirehampton	5 35	6 37	....	7 34	....	7 48	8 34	9 5	9 47	1028	1112	1152
9	Avonmouth Dock (Jt.) arr.	5 39	6 41	7 32	7 38	7 42	....	8 38	9 9	9 51	1032	1116	1156
13½	Severn Beach .... ,,	....	....	7 48	....	....	....	....	....	10 6	....	....	....

Miles	Down.	aft	aft	aft	aft	aft	aft	aft	aft	aft	aft	aft
—	Bristol (Temple Meads) dep.	1215	....	1 5	2 7	....	2 55	3 43	4 13	....	4 55
1	Lawrence Hill	1219	....	1 9	2 11	....	2 59	3 47	4 17	4 33	4 59
1½	Stapleton Road	1222	1237	1 12	2 14	....	3 2	3 50	4 20	4 36	5 2
2¼	Montpelier	1226	1241	1 16	2 18	2 47	3 6	3 54	4 24	4 40	5 6
3¼	Redland	1229	1244	1 19	2 21	2 50	3 9	3 57	4 27	4 43	5 9
4	Clifton Down ...... arr.	1231	1246	1 21	2 23	2 52	3 11	3 59	4 29	4 45	5 11
	Clifton Down ...... dep.	1232	1247	1 23	2 25	2 53	3 13	4 1	4 30	....	5 14
6	Sea Mills	1237	1252	1 28	2 30	2 58	3 18	4 6	4 35	....	5 20
7½	Shirehampton	1242	1257	1 33	3 35	3 3	3 23	4 11	4 40	....	5 26
9	Avonmouth Dock (Jt.) arr.	1246	1 1	1 37	2 39	3 7	3 27	4 15	4 44	....	5 30
13½	Severn Beach .... ,,	....	....	....	2 55	....	....	....	....	....	....

Down.	Week Days—*Continued.* aft	m	aft	aft	aft	aft	aft	aft	aft	aft	aft	aft (Wednesdays & Saturdays.)	Sundays. mrn	aft	aft	aft	aft	a
Bristol (Temple Meads).. .dep.	5 35	5 55	6 10	6 45	7 8	7 30	8 20	8 50	9 15	1010	11 5	....	7 5	2 5	3 25	4 25	6 0	8 55
Lawrence Hill	5 39	6 0	6 14	6 49	7 12	7 34	8 24	8 54	9 19	1014	1110	....	....	....	....	....	....	....
Stapleton Road	5 42	6 4	6 17	6 52	7 15	7 37	8 27	8 57	9 22	1017	1113	....	7 11	2 11	3 31	4 31	6 6	9 1
Montpelier	5 46	6 9	6 21	6 56	7 19	7 41	8 31	9 1	9 26	1021	1117	....	....	2 15	3 35	4 35	6 10	9 5
Redland	5 49	6 12	6 24	6 59	7 22	7 44	8 34	9 4	9 29	1024	....	....	....	....	....	....	....	....
Clifton Down .... arr.	5 51	6 14	6 26	7 1	7 24	7 46	8 36	9 6	9 31	1026	1121	....	7 17	2 19	3 39	4 39	6 14	9 9
Clifton Down .... dep.	5 53	6 15	6 28	7 2	....	7 47	8 38	....	9 33	1028	....	1125	7 19	2 20	3 40	4 40	6 15	9 10
Sea Mills	5 58	6 21	6 33	7 7	....	7 52	8 43	....	9 38	1033	....	....	....	2 25	3 45	4 45	6 20	9 15
Shirehampton	6 3	6 27	6 38	7 12	....	7 57	8 48	....	9 43	1038	....	1137	....	2 30	3 50	4 50	6 25	9 20
Avonmouth Dock (Joint)..arr.	6 7	6 31	6 42	7 16	....	8 1	8 52	....	9 47	1042	....	1141	7 29	2 34	3 54	4 54	6 29	9 24
Severn Beach.......... ,,	6 23	....	....	....	....	....	....	....	....	....	....	....	....	....	....	....	....	....

e Except Saturdays. m Motor Car, one class only. s Saturdays only.
¶ Temple Meads; about 1 mile to St. Philips Station.

BRISTOL, FILTON JUNCTION, and AVONMOUTH DOCK.—Great Western.

Miles	Down.	Week Days only. mrn	mrn	mrn	mrn	S aft	aft	E aft	E aft	aft
	Bristol (Temple Mds.) dep.	6 2	6 50	....	1025	....	1 55	3 50	....	7 0
1	Lawrence Hill	6 7	6 55	....	1029	....	1 59	3 55	....	7 5
1¼	Stapleton Road	6 11	7 0	....	1033	....	2 2	3 59	....	7 8
2¼	Ashley Hill	6 16	7 4	....	1037	....	2 6	4 3	....	7 12
4¾	Filton Junction	6 24	7 12	....	1045	....	2 14	4 11	....	7 20
7¾	Henbury	6 33	7 21	8 33	1054	12 2	2 22	4 18	5 0	7 29
12¾	Avonmouth Dock (Jt.) arr	6 44	7 33	8 45	11 5	1220	2 33	....	5 12	7 40

Miles	Up.	Week Days only. mrn	mrn		S aft	S aft	aft	E aft	aft	aft
	Joint Station, Avonmouth Dock ... dep.	8 22	1110	....	12 10	12 30	2 22	5 18	5 27	6 55
5	Henbury	8 36	1124	....	12h20	12 42	2 34	....	5 42	7 8
8	Filton Junction 62, 67	8 44	1133	....	....	12 51	2 43	....	5 52	7 17
10¼	Ashley Hill	8 49	1138	....	12 37	12 56	2 48	5 39	5 57	7 22
11	Stapleton Road 17, 62	8 53	1141	....	12 40	12 59	2 51	5 44	6 2	7 26
11¾	Lawrence Hill	8 53	1146	....	12 42	1 1	2 53	5 47	6 9	7 31
12¾	Bristol § 12, 17, 62 .. arr.	9 2	1150	....	12a51	....	3 0	5a58	6 13	7 35

• Temple Meads Passengers change at Lawrence Hill. E Except Saturdays. h Stops to set down. m Motor Car, one class only. S Saturdays only.
§ Temple Meads; about 1 mile to St. Philips Station.

October 1923

BRISTOL, FILTON JUNCTION, and AVONMOUTH DOCK.

Miles.	Down.	Week Days only. mrn	mrn	mrn	mrn	mrn	S	aft	aft	aft	aft	aft
	Bristol (Temple Meads)..dep.	6 2	6 50	6 57	..	10 17	1 30	1 55	3 15	E	7 0	..
1	Lawrence Hill	6 7	6 55	7 1	8 29	10 21	1 34	1 59	3 19	4 28	7 5	8 55
1¼	Stapleton Road	6 11	6 59	7 4	8 33	10 24	1 37	2 2	3 22	4 31	7 10	8 58
2¼	Ashley Hill	6 16	7 3	7 8	8 36	10 28	1 41	2 6	3 26	4 35	7 14	9 2
3¾	Horfield	6 20	7 8	..	8 40	10 32	1 45	2 10	3 30	4 39	7 18	9 6
4½	Filton Junction	6 24	7 12	....	8 44	10 36	1 49	2e14	3 34	4 43	7 22	9 10
5¼	North Filton Platform	6 26	....	7 18	8 46	10 39	1 52	2e17	3 37	..	7 25	9 13
8	Henbury	6 33	7 21	....	....	10 45	1 57	2e22	3 43	....	7 31	m
12	St. Andrew's Road	6 42	7 30	..	..	10 54	2 6	2e31	3 52	..	7 40	..
13	Avonmouth Dock (Jt.) arr.	6 45	7 33	....	....	10 57	2 10	2e35	3 55	....	7 43	....

NOTES.

A Temple Meads; about 1 mile to St. Philips Station.
a Temple Meads Passengers change at Stapleton Road.
E or e Except Saturdays.
m Motor Car, one class only.
S Saturdays only.

August 1928

BRISTOL, CLIFTON DOWN, AVONMOUTH DOCK, and ST. ANDREW'S ROAD.

Miles.	Down.	Week Days. mrn	mrn	mrn	mrn	mrn	mrn	mrn m	mrn	mrn	mrn
	Bristol (Temple Meads) dep.	5 10	....	....	....	....	8 2	8 55	10 0	....	1130
1	Lawrence Hill	5 14	....	....	....	....	8 7	8 59	10 4	....	1134
1¼	Stapleton Road	5 17	....	....	....	....	8 10	....	1014	....	1138
2¼	Montpelier	5 21	....	7 8	....	....	8 15	....	1018	....	1142
3¼	Redland	....	....	....	....	....	8 18	....	1021	....	1145
4	Clifton Down arr.	5 25	....	7 12	....	....	8 20	....	1023	....	1147
	Clifton Down dep.	5 26	....	7 15	....	....	8 22	....	1024	....	1148
6	Sea Mills	5 31	....	7 21	....	....	8 28	....	1029	....	1153
7¾	Shirehampton	5 36	....	....	7 32	....	8 34	....	1034	....	1158
9	Avonmouth Dock (Joint)	5 42	7 10	7 32	7 37	8 23	8 40	....	1038	1111	12 2
10	St. Andrew's Road .. arr.	5 45	7 13	7 35	7 40	8 26	8 43	....	....	1114	....

Down.	Week Days. S aft	S aft	aft	aft	aft	aft	aft	E aft	aft	E aft	aft	E aft	aft	aft	aft
Bristol (Temple Meads) dep.	....	....	1210	12s34	1 5	....	....	....	3 45	....	4 52	....	5 55	6 10	....
Lawrence Hill	....	....	1214	12 38	1 9	1 42	....	2 0	3 51	4 33	4 56	5 28	6 0	6 14	6 26
Stapleton Road	....	....	1217	12 42	1 12	1 45	....	2 3	3 55	4 36	4 59	5 30	6 4	6 17	6 30
Montpelier	....	....	1221	12 46	1 16	1 49	....	2 8	3 59	4 40	5 3	....	6 9	6 21	....
Redland	....	....	1224	12 49	1 19	1 52	....	2 11	4 2	4 43	5 5	....	6 12	6 24	....
Clifton Down arr.	....	....	1226	12 51	1 21	1 54	....	2 13	4 4	4 45	5 7	....	6 14	6 26	....
Clifton Down dep.	....	....	1227	12 52	1 23	....	....	2 14	4 6	4 46	5 9	....	6 15	6 27	....
Sea Mills	....	....	1232	12 57	1 28	....	....	2 19	4 11	4 52	5 14	....	6 21	6 32	....
Shirehampton	....	....	1237	1 2	1 33	....	....	2 24	4 16	4 57	5 19	....	6 27	6 37	....
Avonmouth Dock (Joint)	1220	1230	1241	1 6	1 39	....	2 20	2 28	4 20	....	5 25	....	6 31	6 41	....
St. Andrew's Road .. arr.	1223	1233	....	....	1 42	....	2 23	....	....	....	5 31	....	....	....	....

Down.	Week Days—Continued. aft m	aft	aft	aft	aft	aft	aft	aft	aft	aft
Bristol (Temple Meads) dep.	....	7 8	....	8 40	8 55	9 15	9 45	1010	1035	11 5
Lawrence Hill	....	7 12	....	8 44	8 59	9 19	9 49	1014	1040	11 9
Stapleton Road	....	7 15	....	8 47	9 2	9 22	9 52	1017	1044	11 12
Montpelier	....	7 19	8 1	8 51	9 6	9 26	9 56	1021	1048	11 16
Redland	....	7 22	8 4	8 54	9 9	9 29	9 59	1024	1051	....
Clifton Down arr.	....	7 24	8 6	8 56	9 11	9 31	10 1	1026	1053	11 20
Clifton Down dep.	....	7 25	....	8 57	....	9 33	....	1028	1057	11s22
Sea Mills	....	7 30	....	9 2	....	9 38	....	1033	11 3	11s27
Shirehampton	....	7 35	....	9 7	....	9 43	....	1038	11 8	11s32
Avonmouth Dock (Joint)	7 8	7 39	....	9 11	....	9 47	....	1042	1112	11s36
St. Andrew's Road ... arr.	7 11	....	....	....	....	9 52	....	....	....	....

Down.	Sundays. mrn	mrn	mrn	mrn	mrn	A aft	B aft	B aft	A aft
Bristol (Temple Meads) dep.	7 5	8 30	9 10	....	1140	5 5	8 15	9 50	1016
Lawrence Hill	7 8	8 34	9 14	1025	1144	5 9	8 19	9 54	1020
Stapleton Road	7 11	8 37	9 17	1028	1147	5 11	8 22	9 57	1023
Montpelier	7 14	8 41	9 21	1032	1150	....	8 26	10 1	....
Redland	....	....	....	....	....	....	....	....	....
Clifton Down arr.	7 17	8 45	9 25	1036	1157	....	8 30	10 5	....
Clifton Down dep.	7 19	8 46	9 26	....	....	....	8 31	10 6	....
Sea Mills	....	8 51	9 31	....	....	....	8 36	1011	....
Shirehampton	7 26	8 56	9 36	....	....	....	8 41	1016	....
Avonmouth Dock (Joint)	7 30	9 0	9 40	....	....	....	8 45	1020	....
St. Andrew's Road ... arr.	7 33	....	....	....	....	....	....	....	....

NOTES.

A Temple Meads: about 1 mile to St. Philips Station.
B Through Train to Weston-super-Mare, see page 15.
b Through Train to Weston-super-Mare and Taunton, see pages 12 and 16 respectively.

August 1928

BRISTOL, PILNING, SEVERN BEACH, AVONMOUTH DOCK, and BRISTOL.

Miles.		Week Days. mrn	mrn	mrn (Motor Car, one class only.)	mrn	mrn	mrn	mrn	aft	aft	aft	aft
	Bristol (Temple M.)..dep.	6A2	7 10	..	8 37	9 25	..	1045	..	..	..	2 6
1	Lawrence Hill	6A7	7 15	....	8 41	9 29	....	1049	....	....	....	2 11
1¼	Stapleton Road	6 18	7 18		8 44	9 32	..	1052	..	..	..	2 14
2¼	Montpelier	6 23	7 23		8 48	9 36	....	1056	....	....	....	2 18
3¼	Redland	..	7 26		8 51	9 39	..	1059	..	..	..	2 21
4	Clifton Down	6 28	7 30		8 55	9 42	....	11 2	....	....	....	2 25
6	Sea Mills	6 33	7 35		9 0	9 47	..	11 7	..	..	..	2 30
7¾	Shirehampton	6 38	7 40		9 5	9 52	....	1112	....	....	....	2 35
9	Avonmouth Dock ... arr.	6 42	7 44		9 9	9 56	..	1116	..	..	..	2 39
—	Avonmouth Dock ... dep.	....	7 46		9 10	9 58	....	1118	....	....	....	2 41
10	St. Andrew's Road	..	7 50		9 14	10 2	..	1122	..	..	..	2 45
13½	Severn Beach arr.	....	7 57		9 21	10 9	....	1129	....	....	....	2 52
	Severn Beach dep.	..	..	8 7	9 23	..	1025	..	12 5	1 35	..	..
14¼	New Passage Halt	....	....	8 10	9 26	....	1028	....	12 8	1 38	....	....
14¾	Cross Hands Halt	..	..	8 12	9 28	..	1030	..	1210	1 40	..	..
15¾	Pilning (Low Level) ... arr.	....	....	8 15	9 30	....	1032	....	1212	1 42	....	....
—	Pilning (High Level).dep.	..	..	..	9 35	..	1037	⁂	..	1 49	..	..
19¼	Patchway	....	....	8 27	....	....	1047	....	....	....	....	....
20½	Filton Junction	..	..	8 32	..	..	1051	..	..	..	..	..
21½	Horfield	....	....	8 34	....	....	1053	....	....	....	....	....
22¾	Ashley Hill	..	..	8 38	..	..	1056	..	..	..	..	..
23¾	Stapleton Road 17	....	....	8 43	9 51	....	1058	....	....	2 0	2 16	....
24¼	Lawrence Hill	..	..	8 46	10A7	..	11 2	..	..	..	2 20	..
25¼	Bristol B 12, 17 ... arr.	....	....	8 52	1011 A	....	1118 A	....	....	2 12	....	....

	Week Days. S aft	aft	aft	aft	E aft	aft	aft	aft	S aft	aft	aft	aft
Bristol (Temple M.)..dep.	..	..	2 55	4 14	5A3	5 35	..	6 40	..	7 30	..	8 5
Lawrence Hill	2 40	....	2 59	4 18	5 12	5 39	....	6 44	....	7 34	....	8 9
Stapleton Road	2 43	..	3 2	4 21	5 15	5 42	..	6 47	..	7 37	..	8 12
Montpelier	2 47	....	3 6	4 25	5 19	5 46	....	6 51	....	7 41	....	8 16
Redland	2 50	..	3 9	4 28	5 21	5 49	..	6 54	..	7 44	..	8 19
Clifton Down	2 53	....	3 13	4 31	5 24	5 53	....	6 57	....	7 47	....	8 22
Sea Mills	2 58	..	3 18	4 36	5 29	5 58	..	7 2	..	7 52	..	8 27
Shirehampton	3 3	....	3 23	4 41	5 34	6 3	....	7 7	....	7 57	....	8 32
Avonmouth Dock ... arr.	3 7	..	3 27	4 45	5 38	6 7	..	7 11	..	8 1	..	8 36
Avonmouth Dock ... dep.	3 8	....	3 29	4 47	5 39	6s9	....	7 13	....	8 3	....	8 38
St. Andrew's Road	3 12	..	3 33	4 51	5 43	6s13	..	7 17	..	8 7	..	8 42
Severn Beach arr.	3 19	....	3 40	4 58	5 50	6s20	....	7 24	....	8 14	....	8 49
Severn Beach dep.	..	3 25	..	..	..	..	6 38	..	7 45	..	8 35	8 50
New Passage Halt	....	3 28	....	....	....	....	6 41	....	7 48	....	8 38	8 53
Cross Hands Halt	..	3 30	..	..	..	..	6 43	..	7 50	..	8 40	8 55
Pilning (Low Level) ... arr.	....	3 32	....	....	....	....	6 45	....	....	....	8 42	8 57
Pilning (High Level).dep.	..	3 36	..	..	..	..	6 50	..	..	..	..	..
Patchway	....	....	....	....	....	....	6 59	....	....	....	8 51	....
Filton Junction	..	..	..	..	..	..	7 2	..	..	..	8 55	..
Horfield	....	....	....	....	....	....	7 5	....	8 2	....	8 57	....
Ashley Hill	..	..	..	..	..	..	7 8	..	8 5	..	8 59	..
Stapleton Road 17	....	3 49	....	....	....	....	7 10	....	8 7	....	9 2	....
Lawrence Hill	..	4A12	..	..	..	..	7 14	..	8 10	..	9 5	..
Bristol B 12, 17 ... arr.	....	4A16	....	....	....	....	7 21	....	8 28	....	9 12	....

	Sundays. aft	aft	aft	aft	aft	aft
Bristol (Temple M.)..dep.	2 5	3 25	4 20	6 0	..	8 15
Lawrence Hill	2 9	3 29	4 24	6 4	....	8 19
Stapleton Road	2 12	3 32	4 27	6 7	..	8 22
Montpelier	2 16	3 36	4 31	6 11	....	8 26
Redland	..	..	..	..	..	..
Clifton Down	2 21	3 41	4 35	6 16	....	8 31
Sea Mills	2 26	3 46	4 41	6 21	..	8 36
Shirehampton	2 31	3 51	4 46	6 26	....	8 41
Avonmouth Dock ... arr.	2 35	3 55	4 50	6 30	..	8 45
Avonmouth Dock ... dep.	2 37	3 56	4 55	6 31	....	8 46
St. Andrew's Road	..	..	..	6 34	..	..
Severn Beach arr.	2 47	4 6	5 5	6 42	....	8 56
Severn Beach dep.	2 48	..	..	6 44	7 0	9 0
New Passage Halt	2 53	....	....	6 47	7 3	9 3
Cross Hands Halt	2 55	..	..	6 49	7 5	9 5
Pilning (Low Level) ... arr.	....	....	....	6 51	....	....
Pilning (High Level).dep.	..	..	..	..	..	..
Patchway	....	....	....	....	....	....
Filton Junction	..	..	..	..	..	..
Horfield	3 7	....	....	....	7 17	9 17
Ashley Hill	3 10	..	..	..	7 20	9 20
Stapleton Road 17	3 12	....	....	....	7 22	9 22
Lawrence Hill	3 16	..	..	..	7 26	9 26
Bristol B 12, 17 ... arr.	3 20	....	....	....	7 30	9 30

A Change at Stapleton Road. B Change at Lawrence Hill. B Temple Meads; about 1 mile to St. Philips Station. E Except Saturdays. S or s Saturdays only.

August 1928

1. Bristol Temple Meads to Clifton Down
BRISTOL TEMPLE MEADS

1. This southward view is from May 1872 and features the BER offices (centre), its wooden station on the left and the original GWR terminus on the right. Carriage sheds are being built in the right background. Note the wagon turntables and that some tracks are mixed gauge. A gentleman's carriage is on a flat wagon on the left. The cross-sleepered mixed gauge track in the foreground connected with the Bristol Harbour Railway, which was constructed by the GWR and the BER. (C.G.Maggs coll.)

2. In this album we will confine our study of Temple Meads to the terminal platforms, as they were used by most trains to the Avonmouth lines. The GWR pioneered diesel railcars in the 1930s and one of this first generation was recorded attached to an ordinary coach in about 1949, bound for Clifton Down. No. 23 was built in 1940 at Swindon with AEC running gear. (J.Moss/R.S.Carpenter)

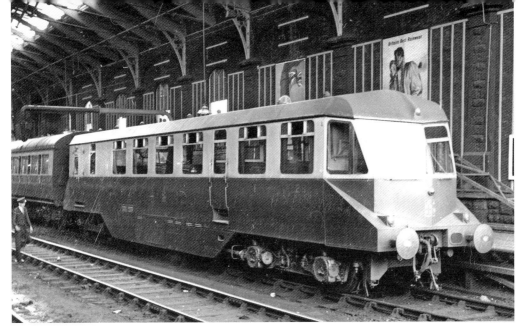

II.　　　Wright's 1912 diagram includes the curved platforms which were built in 1874-78 as part of the GWR/MR Joint station. The BER had one platform on its site from 1845 until which time its trains reversed in and out of the GWR terminus. From that year it also had terminal platforms in the building on the left of the picture above. The shed to cover platforms 5 and 7 was constructed in 1875 and the cost shared by the GWR (3/8), the MR (3/8) and the BER (2/8). The "Approach to UP TRAINS" is still in use, but the road to the down side was lost during the rebuilding of 1933-35, when five more platforms were added. The plan shows five separate booking offices. Platform 3 was added in 1899 and the down bay in 1892, following the end of broad gauge.

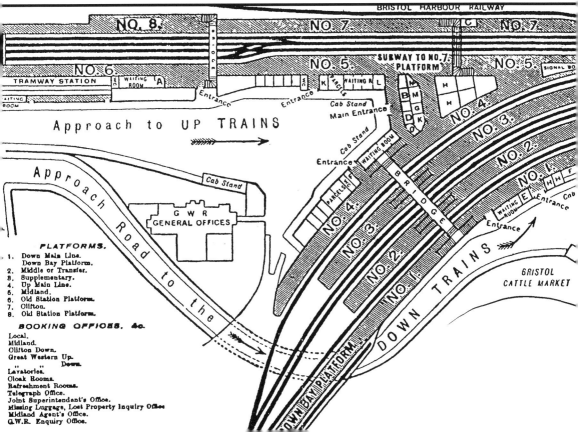

PLATFORMS.

1. Down Main Line.
   Down Bay Platform.
2. Middle or Transfer.
3. Supplementary.
4. Up Main Line.
5. Midland.
6. Old Station Platform.
7. Clifton.
8. Old Station Platform.

BOOKING OFFICES, &c.

Local.
Midland.
Clifton Down.
Great Western Up.
　　　　　　" 　　Down.
Lavatories.
Cloak Rooms.
Refreshment Rooms.
Telegraph Office.
Joint Superintendent's Office.
Missing Luggage, Lost Property Inquiry Office
Midland Agent's Office.
G.W.R. Enquiry Office.

3.　　　The lower part of the train shed in the background is Brunel's original terminus of 1840, the nearer section being completed in 1875. The photograph is from 22nd May 1956, when two of BR's fairly new class 3 2-6-2Ts were in attendance, the one on the right being no.

82004. Behind it is Old Station signal box which controlled only that area and was in use until 12th September 1965, when all the visible tracks were taken out of use. The part of platform 12 behind the camera was retained for Avonmouth DMUs. (P.J.Kelley)

4.　　　The platforms were renumbered in 1934 and again in 1970 when No. 12 became No. 1. A class 119 is departing from it on 23rd May 1981, leaving an unwelcome smokescreen. Behind it are the lines to the freight depot, traffic to which was transferred to Avonmouth on 1st August 1982. Colour light signalling was introduced to the station area on 24th November 1935. (M.Turvey)

5.　　　This is an example of a train for Severn Beach departing from a main line platform, No. 5. It is the 11.55 on 8th August 1991. Under this roof until the 1930s were six platform faces, four through lines and a bay. Abolition of the broad gauge had given space for two island platforms and another bay. (M.J.Stretton)

6.   On the right is platform 1, but it was occupied by a third generation DMU (no. 158866) bound for Worcester Shrub Hill on 28th March 2004 at 15.15. The windows above it are on the 1970 Signalling Centre. This was a Sunday when no trains ran to Severn Beach. At platform 3 (left) is Virgin Voyager no. 220034 departing for Glasgow at 14.58. It has diesel-electric power under each coach and so is regarded as a fourth generation DMU. The bridge above it houses the redundant mailbag conveyor system, last used in 1998. (V.Mitchell)

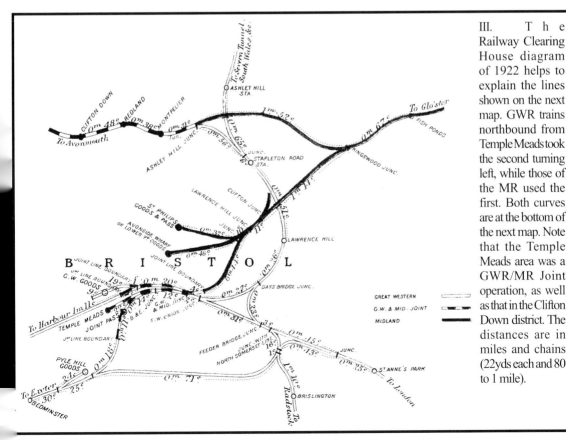

III.   The Railway Clearing House diagram of 1922 helps to explain the lines shown on the next map. GWR trains northbound from Temple Meads took the second turning left, while those of the MR used the first. Both curves are at the bottom of the next map. Note that the Temple Meads area was a GWR/MR Joint operation, as well as that in the Clifton Down district. The distances are in miles and chains (22yds each and 80 to 1 mile).

Views of the other platforms, the entrances and the locomotive sheds can be found in several companion albums. These are listed below the final picture in this volume.

IV.   The 1921 map at 6 ins to 1 mile has the MR's St Philips terminus lower centre on the left page. This was used by most MR trains for Clifton Down or beyond from 1880 to 1897. After that time, the connection north of Lawrence Hill station was removed. The MR to Birmingham runs diagonally across the right page and that company's Clifton Extension is across the top of both, while Montpelier station is just off the left border. Near the join of the pages is a viaduct which was demolished in 1968 to make way for the M32. It was known as "13 Arches Viaduct".

EAST OF TEMPLE MEADS

7. We are looking south across the junction shown at the bottom of map IV in 1931. The line to Temple Meads is on the right. Beyond the signals in the centre are two new lines which would become part of the quadruple track after the signal box was demolished and the other pair laid on its site. The original alignment was resumed in 1970. The curve on the left was named Bristol Loop Line and opened on 29th May 1886. It was quadruple track from September 1891 to May 1965.
(Brunel University/ Mowat coll.)

8. From the same bridge, we see Dr. Day's Bridge Junction on 12th October 1965, as class 9F no. 92213 hauls freight from the Bath direction. The quadruple track curve came into use in January 1933. Centre is the hut which appears in both pictures. The replacement signal box was behind the camera and was in use until 9th March 1970.
(T.Heavyside)

LAWRENCE HILL

9.   The single track was doubled in 1873 and this was quadrupled to Dr. Day's Bridge Junction in 1891. This northward view is from the Edwardian era and approaching is an 0-6-0ST. (Lens of Sutton)

10.   A southward panorama from the 1960s includes the 38-lever signal box which was in use from 1890 to 1970. The main lines are on the left and the relief lines are in the foreground. (N.C.Simmons)

11.   The trackbed of the main lines is on the left of this 1999 southward view. The rails had been in use until 1984, but there had been only double track beyond the station since 1970. The curve on the right had been opened in February 1970 to serve Avonside Wharf. There had been a goods yard in the centre of the view until the mid-1980s. A cement terminal continued for another ten years. (V.Mitchell)

12.   Crossing the former MR bridge from which the previous picture was taken, we see the Avonside Wharf line on the left, which had only been used by refuse trains since November 1985. The undergrowth on the left covers the site of the MR/GWR double track connection used between 1880 and 1897. The bridge carried Easton Road, after which the junction was named. (V.Mitchell)

STAPLETON ROAD

13.   The station had one platform from 1863 to 1874, two until 1888 and four until 1971, after which time only two were used. Quadrupling southwards took place in November 1891; this view is in that direction. There was a refreshment room on the island platform. (Lens of Sutton)

14.   Looking north in 1963, we have the main lines on the right. This was the only Bristol stopping point for trains between the South Coast and South Wales in the steam era. Its long platforms were thus very busy at times, but only a short part of those on the left have been used in recent years, mainly for local trains. (Stations UK)

15.　　The main building was on the east side and was recorded in 1964. All structures were subsequently demolished, leaving only an exposed footbridge visible in the background of picture 17. (M.Oakley coll.)

NORTH OF STAPLETON ROAD

16.　　This is Narroways Hill Junction, where the Clifton Down route curves to the right. Stapleton Road station is in the distance and on the right is its goods yard, which closed on 29th November 1965. Partially obscured by three poles on the left is the 1920 signal box, which had 102 levers and closed on 19th October 1970. Also on the left is the gasworks siding, which was in use from 1878 to 1973, although gas production ceased in 1971. It also had a connection to the former MR route. (LGRP/NRM)

17.   We have another view from the MR's embankment for the Fishponds line, but this is from August 1986. The railcar is bound for Avonmouth on the line which was singled on 19th October 1970. The main line was reduced to double track on 20th February 1984. (P.G.Barnes)

18.   Ashley Hill Junction came into being when the MR opened its line from Fishponds in 1874. An 0-4-4T from there is seen in about 1910 approaching the 1904 signal box, which was in use until 10th May 1959. It was replaced by one with a flat roof and 23 levers; this lasted until 27th February 1966. The route was singled temporarily on 30th March 1941, following bomb damage, and closed completely on 14th June 1965. (LGRP/G.A.Nicholls coll.)

MONTPELIER

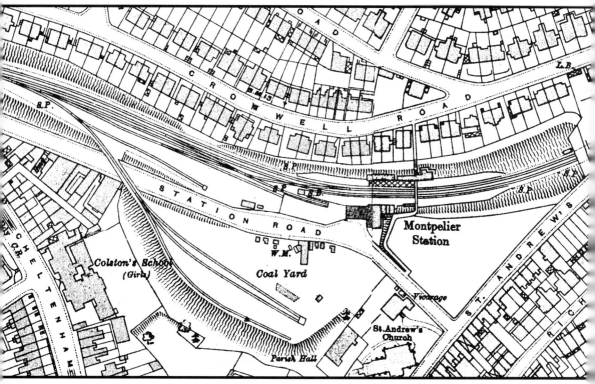

V.   The 1918 survey shows that the area north of the station was developed with houses mostly larger than those on the lower ground, reflecting the social levels of the 1870s. The station opened on 1st October 1874.

19.   A 1928 record includes the signal box, which had 16 levers and closed on 10th May 1959. The adjacent goods yard was in use until 29th November 1965. The station house (left) was destroyed during an air raid on 16th March 1941. (Brunel University/Mowat coll.)

20.   An eastward panorama from the 1960s has the portal of Montpelier Tunnel (288 yards) in the distance. The footbridge gave access to Station Road and Cromwell Road - see map. The canopy was added in 1896. The staffing levels fell from 19 in 1903 to 15 in 1938. The insert shows the station in more detail. (Stations UK)

21.   The coal yard was unusual in that access to it was by way of a bridge. Look on the right. There is now no trace of either. A ground frame was provided from 1959 to 1966. This view is from Cheltenham Road Viaduct. The engine shunting the yard is BR class 5 no. 73080, which was normally based at Eastleigh. (D.J.Cross)

22.	A 1957 picture includes a Standard 8 and a Sunbeam Talbot. The wing on the right was a post-war structure. The station was staffed until 17th July 1967. (M.Oakley coll.)

23.	The building was in commercial use when photographed in June 2004. The line had been singled on 19th October 1970. (V.Mitchell)

REDLAND

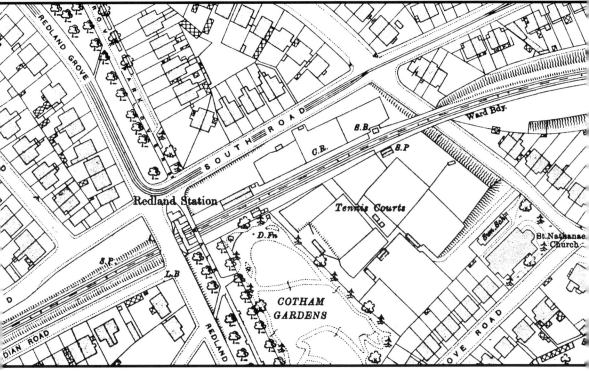

VI.   The 1916 survey includes the signal box (S.B.), which was officially open from 1899 to 1950, but only at peak holiday times. Its last recorded use was in 1936. The station opened on 12th April 1897 after much local lobbying.

24.   The down platform waiting room is in the background as the staff pose. A total of 11 men were employed in 1903, which had fallen to just six in 1938. (M.Oakley coll.)

25.　　The nearest bridge carries Grove Park Walk, its tree-lined route being shown top to bottom on the map. Between it and the road bridge is the footbridge linking the platforms to the booking office, top right. These were demolished in about 1973 and the boards have subsequently been removed from the fine ironwork. (Lens of Sutton coll.)

26.　　A 1960 photo features 4300 class 2-6-0 no. 6319, by then an unusual sight, as most trains were diesel operated on this route by that time. It is at the down platform, which was taken out of use in 1970. The up building was still standing in 2004, although unstaffed since 1967. Platform access was at its far end and was at road level. (E.T.Gill/R.K.Blencowe)

27.　　The booking office is visible on the left as no. 3816 heads for Clifton Down in August 1963 with stock for a return Zoo excursion. Most such trains were from South Wales, this necessitating a reversal and change of engine at Pilning, Stoke Gifford, Stapleton Road or Temple Meads. (D.J.Cross)

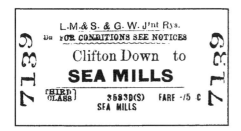

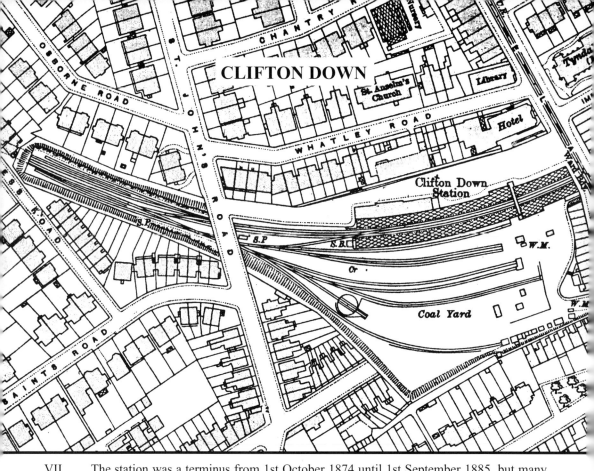

VII.   The station was a terminus from 1st October 1874 until 1st September 1885, but many trains terminated here thereafter, hence the turntable on this 1916 map. On the left is Clifton Down Tunnel, 1751 yds in length.

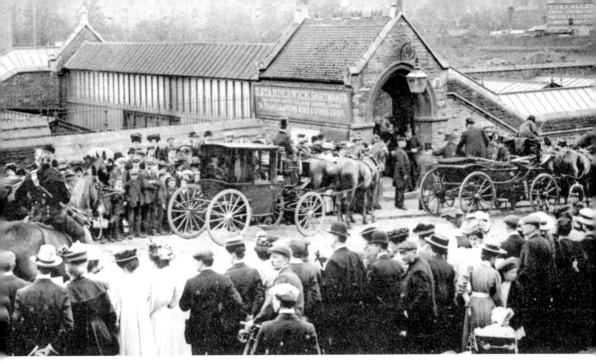

(lower left)

28.   This photograph is from prior to 1908 and includes both GWR and MR trains. The MR service between here and Fishponds was suspended between 1st January 1917 and 5th May 1919, final withdrawal coming on 31st March 1941, again due to wartime factors. (Stations UK)

29.   The splendid footbridge was recorded on 15th May 1907, when several Empire Prime Ministers arrived to visit the docks under construction at Avonmouth. The bridge is in the left background of pictures 28, 32 and 35. The archway was still in use in 2004. The station employed an average of 22 people from 1903 through to the 1930s. (M.Oakley coll.)

30.   The office of Davey's Clifton Pantechnicons is in the background of picture no. 28 and this is part of the company's fleet of such vehicles. They were recorded in the goods yard attached to no. 2321, a MR Kirtley 0-6-0. (P.Davey coll.)

31.   The high standard of finish is evident in this 1956 picture. Clifton Zoo brought many excursion trains to this station, particularly from the valleys of South Wales. There were also excursion trains from here to Ashton Gate (for football), to Weston-super-Mare, to the South Coast and to London. (H.C.Casserley)

32. The signal box was recorded on 21st July 1967; its 28 lever frame was in use until 18th October 1970, when the branch was singled. However, a passing loop was provided here. The box had been extended towards us in World War I, hence the locking room window being offset to the right. (C.L.Caddy)

33. Parts of the canopies were lost during the 1930s and the remainder was removed in May 1971. Photographed in May 1959, the goods yard closed on 5th July 1965. The yard had a crane capable of lifting up to 5 tons; it is right of centre. (P.J.Garland/R.S.Carpenter)

34.   The main building on the up side was retained and it has served a number of different catering purposes since staffing ceased in 1967. This is a 1973 view. (T.J.Edgington)

35.   A 2004 eastward view shows the back of a row of shops that was built on a concrete raft above the tracks in the 1960s and a large shopping complex (right) that was erected in part of the goods yard subsequently. The ramp was then a recent addition. (V.Mitchell)

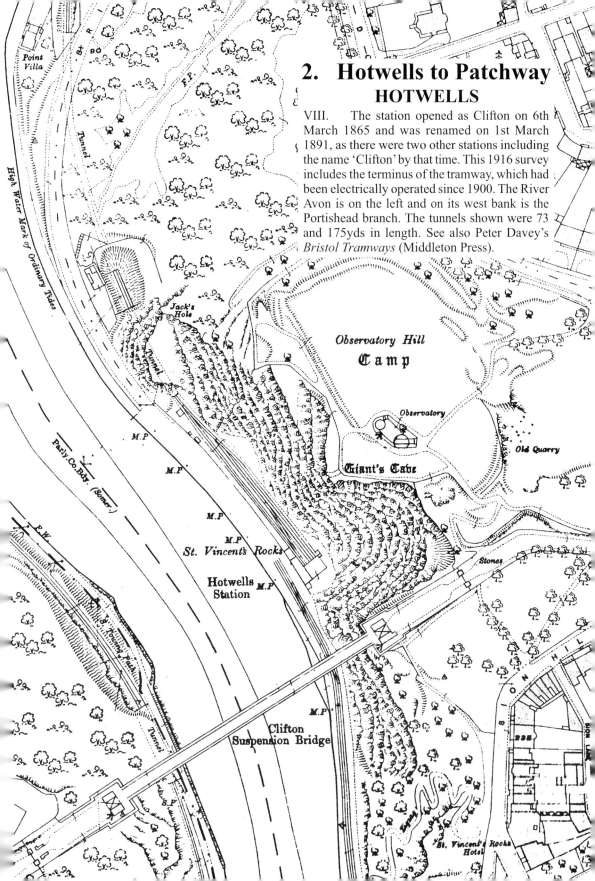

2. Hotwells to Patchway
HOTWELLS

VIII.   The station opened as Clifton on 6th March 1865 and was renamed on 1st March 1891, as there were two other stations including the name 'Clifton' by that time. This 1916 survey includes the terminus of the tramway, which had been electrically operated since 1900. The River Avon is on the left and on its west bank is the Portishead branch. The tunnels shown were 73 and 175yds in length. See also Peter Davey's *Bristol Tramways* (Middleton Press).

Point Villa

Tunnel

High Water Mark of Ordinary Tides

Jack's Hole

Tunnel

Observatory Hill
Camp

Observatory

Old Quarry

M.P

M.P

Party Co. Bdy. (Somer.)

M.P

Giant's Cave

M.P

M.P
St. Vincent's Rocks

Stones

Hotwells Station   *M.P*

Tunnel

Towing path

M.P

ION HILL

Clifton Suspension Bridge

St. Vincent's Rocks Hotel

36. This photograph is probably from about 1870, when the railway was still isolated from all others and passengers had to reach the station along the river bank. The three lines converge on a turntable, which was removed in about 1890. The centre track was used for run-round purposes and the left one was for carriage storage. The bridge was completed in December 1864 as a memorial to I.K.Brunel who had submitted a design for it in his young days. (M.Oakley coll.)

37. The booking office was on the ground floor and internal stairs led to the door seen in the previous picture. There was a refreshment room at platform level until 1893. Dock workers were regular users of this station. The staff usually comprised a station master and a porter.
(M.Oakley coll.)

38.	A view from the bridge shows the final layout before closure on 19th September 1921. The site was required for the construction of a road to Avonmouth, which eventually became the A4. (H.C.Leat/M.Oakley coll.)

HOTWELLS HALT

39.	The short platform at Hotwells could not cope with the enormous number of munition workers travelling to Avonmouth towards the end of World War I. This is the only record available of the platform, which opened on 14th May 1917 and outlasted the terminus, closing on 3rd July 1922. It was situated at the top edge of the map and north of it was a run-round loop.
(S.Loxton/M.Oakley coll.)

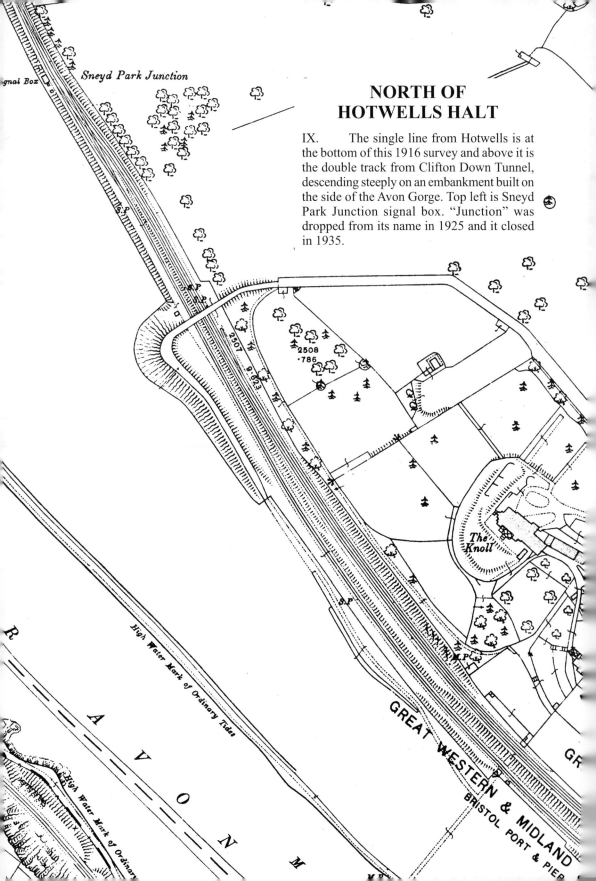

Sneyd Park Junction

gnal Box

NORTH OF HOTWELLS HALT

IX.   The single line from Hotwells is at the bottom of this 1916 survey and above it is the double track from Clifton Down Tunnel, descending steeply on an embankment built on the side of the Avon Gorge. Top left is Sneyd Park Junction signal box. "Junction" was dropped from its name in 1925 and it closed in 1935.

2507
9.623
2508
.786

The Knoll

High Water Mark of Ordinary Tides

R

A V O N

High Water Mark of Ordinary

High Water Mark of Ordinary Tides

GREAT WESTERN & MIDLAND
BRISTOL PORT & PIER

GR

40.　　This photograph, looking down the Avon Gorge towards Avonmouth, must have been taken between 1867 and 1873, when the inclined plane was in place to transport spoil from the dock and river improvement works to fill in quarries on Durdham Downs. The original track is still in place on the Port and Pier Railway; the sleepers were long enough to accommodate broad gauge should it be sold to the GWR or Bristol & Exeter Railways! Much of the material came from the Cumberland Basin and was hauled up the incline by a stationary steam engine.
(G.A.Nicholls coll.)

January 1901

BRISTOL, CLIFTON DOWN, HOTWELLS, and AVONMOUTH.—Great Western & Midland

(Railway timetable, Down trains — first section)

Down.																									
2 Bath (Manvers St.)		6 20					8 22	9 0	9 45			1025	1110		1134	12 5	12 4½	1 5		1 33	2 1
Bristol (Temple Md.) dp	6 45	7 5	7 50	8 37	9 7	9 50	1010	1045	1123	1148	1225	1252	1 10	1 45	2 20	3 0
Lawrence Hill	6 50	7 10	7 54	8 41	9 11	9 54	1014	1050	1127	1152	1229	1256	1 14	1 49	2 26	3 6
Stapleton Road	6 54	7 14	7 57	8 44	9 14	9 57	1017	1054	1132	1156	1232	1 1	1 17	1 53	2 30	3 9
Montpelier	6 59	7 18	8 1	8 48	9 18	10 2	1021	1059	1136	12 0	1236	1 6	1 21	1 57	2 35	3 14
Redland	7 2	7 21	8 4	8 51	9 21	10 5	1024	11 2	1139	12 3	1239	1 9	1 24	2 0	2 38	3 17
Clifton Down {arr.	7 4	7 23	8 6	8 53	9 23	10 7	1026	11 4	1141	12 5	1241	1 11	1 26	2 2	2 40	3 19
{dep.		7 24					10 8		Stop			1 12			2 43
Hotwells dep.		7 10		8 40					1120		1240				2 25
Sea Mills				8 43			1018		1129		1249		1 22		2 34	2 52
Shirehampton	7 26	7 38	8 56		1023	1136	1256	1 28	2 41	2 59
Avonmouth Dock	7 33	7 44	9 1	1028	1142	1 2	1 33	2 47	3 4
Avonmouth arr.	7 35	7 46	9 3	1030	1145	1 5	1 35	2 50	3 6

(Down trains — second section)

Down.																								
4 Bath (Manvers St.)	3 18	3 5	3 38	4 26	4 40	5 12	6 0	6 42	7 0	8 0	8 16	830	9 2	9 50	1020	
Bristol (Temple Md.) dp	3 40	4 20	4 55	5 23	5 45	6 10	6 45	7 10	7 45	8 30	8 55	9 30	9 55	1020	1055
Lawrence Hill	3 40	3 44	4 24	4 59	5 27	5 49	6 14	6 50	7 14	7 49	8 34	8 59	9 34	9 59	1025	1059
Stapleton Road	3 45	3 47	4 27	5 2	5 30	5 52	6 17	6 55	7 17	7 53	8 38	9 3	9 37	10 2	1025	11 3
Montpelier	3 51	4 31	5 6	5 34	5 56	6 22	7 0	7 22	7 58	8 43	8 9	9 42	10 6	1034	11 8
Redland	3 54	4 34	5 9	5 37	5 59	6 25	7 3	7 25	8 1	8 46	11 9	9 45	10 9	1037	1111
Clifton Down {arr.	3 56	4 36	5 11	5 39	6 1	6 27	7 5	7 27	8 3	8 48	9 13	9 47	1011	1039	1113
{dep.				5 40			Stop	7 28		8 50						1120
Hotwells dep.		4 30	5 35			7 10		8 40	
Sea Mills		4 39	5 42	5 51		7 19	7 38	8 48	9 0	
Shirehampton	4 46	5 48	5 57	7 26	7 43	8 52	9 7	1132
Avonmouth Dock	4 51	5 53	6 2	7 30	7 48	9 13	1138
Avonmouth arr.	4 53	5 55	6 4	7 32	7 50	9 15	1140

SEA MILLS

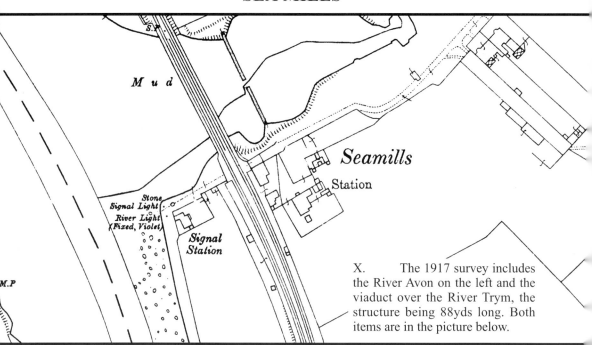

X. The 1917 survey includes the River Avon on the left and the viaduct over the River Trym, the structure being 88yds long. Both items are in the picture below.

41.　　　This postcard features the down platform which dates from 1907 when the line was doubled. No footbridge was provided, but there was a subway for some years. It was prone to flooding and unsavoury deposits. In 1923 staffing levels peaked at this station where they remained until 1935 at a total of six. (Lens of Sutton coll.)

42.　　　A 1964 photo includes part of the 1894 station house (right) and beyond it is the 1906 up building, which included a booking office and a waiting room. The down side was taken out of use upon singling in 1970. The signals near the station were motor worked from Shirehampton and Clifton Down. (Stations UK)

43.   A class 158 DMU passes through on 26th June 2004, working a diverted Cardiff to Portsmouth Harbour service. Two shelters were available for local passengers and the crossing was used for a public path. (V.Mitchell)

44.   The entrance to the platform in 2004 was to the right of the main building, which was then used as offices. To the left is the house once occupied by the station master. (V.Mitchell)

SHIREHAMPTON

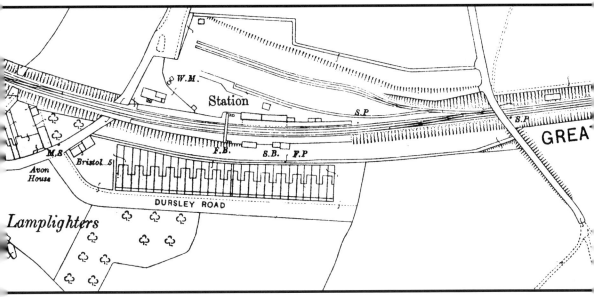

XI.   The map is from 1916 and includes the house for the station master, near the weighing machine (W.M.). A fourth siding was added in 1921 and extended across the road to the yard of R.Brodie, for the conveyance of materials for the construction of the Portway Road. The private siding lasted until 1985, having served a domestic fuel oil store since 1980.

45.   The goods yard is seen in an indifferent photograph from 1928; its traffic ceased on 29th November 1965. The station employed on average ten men during the 1930s.
(Brunel University/Mowat coll.)

46. An east-ward view from May 1959 includes the goods yard points and the last surviving building of the BPR&PC (left). It housed the company's headquarters and superintendents office, the adjacent building being added by the GWR in 1893. There was an engine shed and a carriage shed in the right distance in the early years. (P.J.Garland/ R.S.Carpenter)

47. The signal box and the wide footbridge were recorded in about 1963. The former had 20 levers and was in use until 18th October 1970, when this part of the line was singled. (C.L.Caddy coll.)

48. Staffing ceased in 1967 and eventually a traditional style shelter was built. A class 158 unit runs through on 26th June 2004, bound for Cardiff having been diverted while working the 10.24 from Portsmouth Harbour. (V.Mitchell)

SOUTH OF AVONMOUTH

49.   A view from the north footpath of the Avon Motorway Bridge on 17th September 1975 features the West Town sidings. The inspection coach in the foreground hauled by no. 31112 waits for the Rowntrees train hauled by no. 46003 (visible in the background) to clear its movement from the siding adjacent to the Avonmouth Dock station. Also visible are redundant Port of Bristol Authority internal use wagons, a remarkable collection of secondhand vehicles from pre-Grouping railways. With the widening of the M5 Avon Bridge, the footpath on this side was abolished and noise reduction barriers removed this view from ordinary cars. The area is lower right on the next map. (G.A.Nicholls)

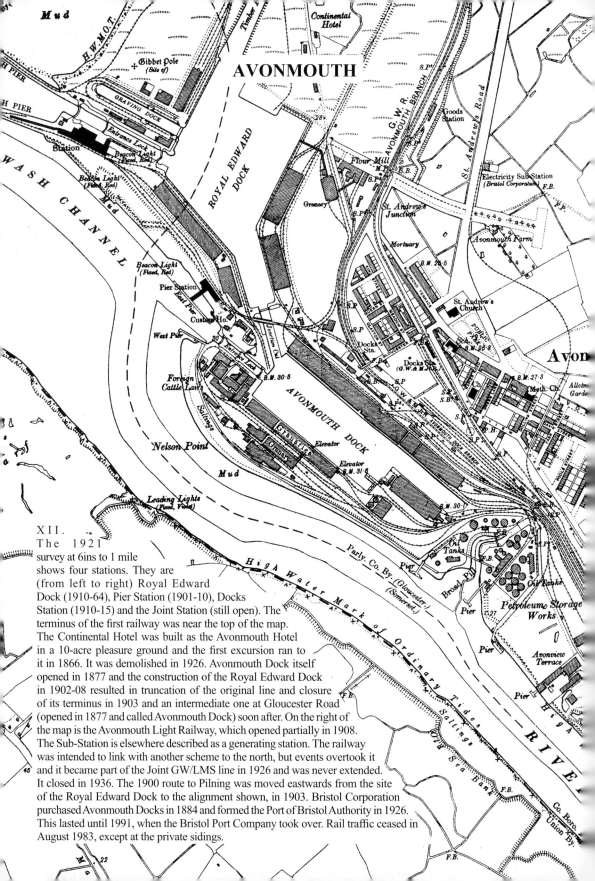

XII.
The 1921 survey at 6ins to 1 mile shows four stations. They are (from left to right) Royal Edward Dock (1910-64), Pier Station (1901-10), Docks Station (1910-15) and the Joint Station (still open). The terminus of the first railway was near the top of the map. The Continental Hotel was built as the Avonmouth Hotel in a 10-acre pleasure ground and the first excursion ran to it in 1866. It was demolished in 1926. Avonmouth Dock itself opened in 1877 and the construction of the Royal Edward Dock in 1902-08 resulted in truncation of the original line and closure of its terminus in 1903 and an intermediate one at Gloucester Road (opened in 1877 and called Avonmouth Dock) soon after. On the right of the map is the Avonmouth Light Railway, which opened partially in 1908. The Sub-Station is elsewhere described as a generating station. The railway was intended to link with another scheme to the north, but events overtook it and it became part of the Joint GW/LMS line in 1926 and was never extended. It closed in 1936. The 1900 route to Pilning was moved eastwards from the site of the Royal Edward Dock to the alignment shown, in 1903. Bristol Corporation purchased Avonmouth Docks in 1884 and formed the Port of Bristol Authority in 1926. This lasted until 1991, when the Bristol Port Company took over. Rail traffic ceased in August 1983, except at the private sidings.

Early Stations

50.   The original 1865 terminus of the Bristol Port Railway & Pier Company is visible behind the wooden fence which separates the line to Avonmouth Dock station from the single line of the Avonmouth and Pilning route of 1900. The construction works in the foreground are for the Royal Edward Dock. In the background can be made out the dark targets of the rifle ranges that for many years provided the main source of passenger revenue at this station. The BPR&P station ceased to be used in May 1903 dating the photograph as 1902-03. (G.A.Nicholls coll.)

51.   This is the only known photograph of the short-lived GWR terminus adjacent to the western Gloucester Road Crossing. It was opened in connection with the rail motor service over the Henbury line in May 1910. This service ceased as an economy measure in 1915 and the terminus closed. (A.H.Hack)

Avonmouth Dock

52.   The 1885 Joint Station was photographed in about 1913, when it had a staff of 25, plus 47 on goods traffic. By 1938, the figures were 38 and 54 respectively. The up platform was added on the extreme right in 1918. The footbridge in the background was used by the photographers taking pictures 53, 54 and 57. The timber building was replaced by brick structures in 1926.
(Lens of Sutton coll.)

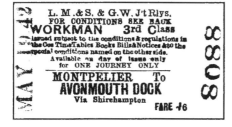

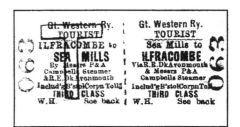

53.   A view towards Bristol on 26th August 1956 shows the station at its optimum with the 1918 platform on the left. The crossover was used by the engines of the many trains that terminated here. (R.M.Casserley)

54.   Looking north in 1959, we see one of the then new DMUs arriving from Severn Beach. There had been two carriage sidings on the left between about 1924 and 1957. Local goods traffic ceased on 20th June 1966. (M.J.Stretton coll.)

55.   A 1964 panorama includes the long bay platform on the left. It had a run-round line from 1904 until it ceased to be used in 1966. Its siding was reinstated for Rowntree Mackintosh in 1971 and used until 1987. (Stations UK)

56.   A return excursion from Clifton Zoo passes through the station on 20th June 1963. Banana vans fill the background and the signal box can be seen on the left. (D.J.Cross)

57.   The signal box was in use from 1903 to January 1969. It had 36 levers when it closed and was known as Avonmouth Dock Passenger signal box. Avonmouth Dock Sidings box (1911-1969. 56 levers) was near the right border of the map and Avonmouth Dock Junction was further south (1911-1988. 26 levers). Ignore the ugly block building. (C.L.Caddy)

58.   Situated in the background of this 1971 photo had been a locomotive shed from 1905 to about 1920. A turntable is shown on the map. The crossing gates (under the camera) were replaced by full lifting barriers in September 1973. They are at the east end of Gloucester Road. (T.J.Edgington)

59.   Seen on 26th June 2004 are two Virgin Voyager units which have been diverted on their journey from Newcastle to Plymouth. The parcels office on the right of the previous picture is on the left of this one; it was used by hairdressers in 2004. (V.Mitchell)

60.   BPA Peckett 0-6-0ST no. S11 *Bristol* is collecting empty stock to form a boat train. On the right are the "Corporation Lines" which acted as a bypass to the station until 1967. The last banana train left on 6th February 1967, the vans often standing in the sidings on the left. These were ex-MR and Joint, four of each. (D.J.Cross)

61.   Looking from the other side of the same footbridge on 26th August 1956, we see part of the triangular connection which leads to the swing bridge over Junction Cut. The locomotive is no. 6671, an 0-6-2T. (H.C.Casserley)

Royal Edward Dock

62.   The Port of Bristol Authority built this fine station and it was opened during a royal visit on 8th July 1908, regular traffic starting on 20th April 1910. This is the east elevation in about 1920. (PBA)

63.   One of the PBA's Peckett 0-6-0STs is ready to depart and it will soon cross the swing bridge over Junction Cut. If bound for London, a GWR loco would usually take the train via Henbury and Badminton in a little over two hours. The station was partially destroyed by bombs in 1941 and the last boat train left on 26th August 1964. The dock still had one siding in 2004. (PBA)

Other Dock Lines

64.   Much of the 31½ miles of the PBA railway had the rails level with the road. A photo from the top of the BOCM (Bristol Oil and Cake Mills) building shows S10 *Hallen* with an internal transfer movement with the side view of the Junction Lock Bridge in the Summer of 1961. The large boat in the background is one of the Clan Line boats bringing refrigerated meat from New Zealand. (G.A.Nicholls)

65.   *Edward* was built by Peckett in 1914 and served its entire career in Bristol Docks until scrapped in 1957. This firm provided 16 other locos for use here over the years and seven from Avonside were also used. The Bristol Docks (BD) stock for internal use was an assortment of secondhand items. (R.S.Carpenter)

66.	A trio of Pecketts was recorded near the 1954 engine shed on 8th July 1965. They are S13 *Redland*, S9 *Henbury* and S12 *Clifton*. This shed was built immediately west of the triangle. Steam operation ceased on PBA lines in August 1965 with the withdrawal of *Redland*. *Henbury* is preserved at the Bristol Industrial Museum. (T.David/C.L.Caddy)

67.	Diesels were introduced progressively, a total of 27 being employed here. The oldest was built in 1950 and the newest in 1965. This is Rolls Royce no. 38 and is seen near the northern end of the PBA system on 12th February 1975, waiting to cross over the BR Severn Beach line to reach the Chittening Factory Estate. Geographically this picture comes after no. 77, but is included here to be within the PBA section. (G.A.Nicholls)

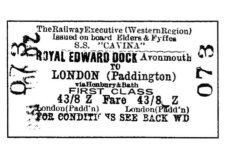

The Railway Executive (Western Region)
Issued on board Elders & Fyffes
S.S. "CAVINA"
ROYAL EDWARD DOCK Avonmouth
TO
LONDON (Paddington)
via Henbury & Bath
FIRST CLASS
43/8 Z	Fare	43/8 Z
London(Padd'n)	London(Padd'n)
FOR CONDITIONS SEE BACK WD

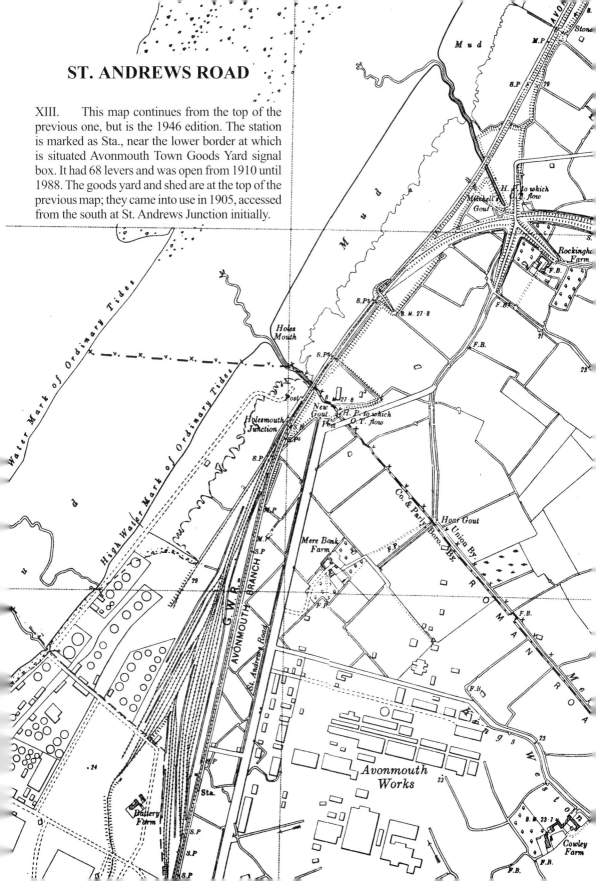

ST. ANDREWS ROAD

XIII.   This map continues from the top of the previous one, but is the 1946 edition. The station is marked as Sta., near the lower border at which is situated Avonmouth Town Goods Yard signal box. It had 68 levers and was open from 1910 until 1988. The goods yard and shed are at the top of the previous map; they came into use in 1905, accessed from the south at St. Andrews Junction initially.

68.   A southward view from 1932 has the Royal Edward sidings on the right and Avonmouth Town Goods Yard box in the distance. The long shelter had been provided for World War I munition workers waiting for trains home. (Brunel University/Mowat coll.)

69.   Looking south again, but in the late 1950s, we see the extra shelters added in the next conflict. The junction and signalling had been altered in 1941 in connection with new sidings for a Ministry of Works Cold Store for emergency food supplies. (Lens of Sutton coll.)

70.	Running across the 1964 picture are buckets conveying zinc ore from ships to the National Smelting Company's works. A vast array of fuel tanks grew up along the coastline. Butane and propane are brought by rail from Wytch Farm oilfield (see our *Swanage to Wareham* album) for export, mainly to Spain. (Stations UK)

71.	No. D1560 waits for a Severn Beach local train to pass before leaving Royal Edward Yard with an oil train on 12th February 1974. The platforms of St. Andrews Road station are on the right. The two running lines to the left were still owned and maintained by the Port of Bristol Authority until closure of the yard in 1977. They were opened in 1911 and are included in pictures 60-61 and 75. (G.A.Nicholls)

72.   St. Andrews Junction Signal Box was photographed on 21st June 1974. This 1910 box remained unchanged on the outside in 2004 and controlled the level crossing from which this view was taken. This is on the principal road access to the docks. The box also housed the satellite panel installed in 1988, when the other signal boxes in the area were closed. (G.A.Nicholls)

73.   Two photographs from 26th June 2004 include massive stockpiles of imported coal, unloaded at Royal Portbury Dock and transported here by conveyor belts which are partially in a tunnel under the Avon estuary. The coal terminal came into use in September 1993; coal has also been loaded subsequently at new sidings at Royal Portbury Dock - see *Branch Lines to Clevedon & Portishead*. Only the former down line remained for passenger use. The adjacent one was for loco release from the three parallel hopper loading lines. The nearest gantry was an unused relic; the others were used for lighting. (V.Mitchell)

74.   Turning round, we find the Severn Beach line near the signal on the left and the sidings packed with empty wagons as coal movement had stopped for two weeks to allow main line diversions mentioned earlier. The loco siding is on the right and out of view are sidings for Hydro-Agri, Rhone Poulenc and Britannia Zinc. (V.Mitchell)

NORTH OF ST. ANDREWS ROAD

75.   This is a 1959 view north from the northern end of Bristol Corporation's double track goods line. They are beyond the signal post and the passenger lines are beyond the fence. Holesmouth Junction box is in the distance and Hallen Marsh Junction is beyond the bridge. The lines in the foreground are on the 1900-03 alignment of the route to Pilning. (P.J.Garland/ R.S.Carpenter)

76.   The 46-lever Holesmouth Junction box dates from 1941, being a replacement for the 1910 structure destroyed in an air raid. It was photographed in 1974 and closed on 25th January 1988. (G.A.Nicholls)

HALLEN MARSH JUNCTION

XIV. Hallen Marsh Junction is marked on the left of this 1ins to 1 mile map of 1946; Holesmouth Junction is shown on the previous map. Our journey continues north and then runs southeast to Patchway. Part 3 of this album is across the centre of the page and down the right border. Northeast of Hallen Marsh Junction is Chittening Factory Estate which had sidings from 1917 to 1927, connected from the north at the 13-lever Chittening Junction signal box. Fresh lines were laid down in 1951, with a link from the dock lines via a flat crossing - see picture 67.

77.   Looking north from the bridge seen in picture 75, we have a panorama of Hallen Marsh Junction with no. 31294 partially obscuring the lines to Fison's fertiliser works and the smelting works. In the background, the lines curve right to Filton Junction, via Henbury. The signal box had a 65-lever frame and was open from 1917 to 1988. The tankers snake off the single line from Severn Beach and obscure the lines to the many firms on the Chittening Estate. Traffic on them ceased in 1983. (T.Heavyside)

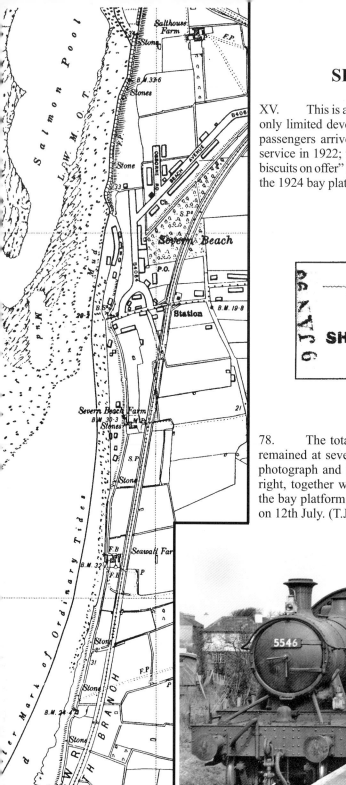

SEVERN BEACH

XV.   This is a continuation from map XIII and shows only limited development as late as 1946. Over 10,000 passengers arrived during the first weekend of public service in 1922; there were "no toilets and only tea and biscuits on offer" it was reported. Curiously, the map omits the 1924 bay platform, signal box and carriage sidings.

B. P. R. & P.
CLIFTON
(HOTWELLS)
TO
SHIREHAMPTON
THIRD CLASS

6 JAN 10

5097

78.   The total number of employees at the station remained at seven from 1923 to 1938. This is a 1950 photograph and it has the 1900 line to Pilning on the right, together with the level crossing. No. 5546 is in the bay platform with the 12.7pm departure for Bristol on 12th July. (T.J.Edgington)

79.   A view in the other direction in August 1956 includes two sidings. They were mainly used for carriage storage, but goods facilities were listed until 10th June 1963. (H.C.Casserley)

80.   A substantial building with sheltered concourse was completed in 1924, but the structures were remote from the platform and parallel to the road. The standard folding trellis barrier was situated centrally under the roof. (Lens of Sutton coll.)

81.   The line in the foreground carried passengers to and from Pilning from 1928 until 1964. Behind the railings is the access path and at the end of the lengthy platform is the 32-lever signal box, which closed on 7th December 1969 and was photographed in October 1965. (C.L.Caddy)

82.   The road frontage and intricate railings were recorded in May 1971. More than 8000 people came during the first Easter of operation (1923), but there was little more than sea breezes and mud initially. A sea-water tank and some other amusements were soon added. (T.J.Edgington)

83.   Day excursions were run by the LMS in the 1930s from the Bristol area, Redditch, Great Malvern, Birmingham and Gloucester. The "resort" declined in popularity in the 1960s and the station building (left) was unstaffed from 1967. Sidings were laid southeast of the station to serve ICI's Severnside Works, which produced fertiliser. These lines were in use from 30th January 1964 until 23rd March 1992. No. 31294 has just run round a train from the works on 27th April 1982 and waits for the DMU to depart at 17.24. (T.Heavyside)

84.   Service was provided by "Pacer" no. 143620 on 20th March 1999. Even the buffers have disappeared since and houses had already been erected on the site of the station building. (M.Turvey)

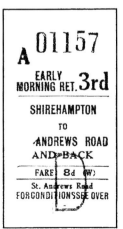

A 01157

EARLY
MORNING RET. 3rd

SHIREHAMPTON
TO
ANDREWS ROAD
AND BACK

FARE 8d (W)
St. Andrews Road
FOR CONDITIONS SEE OVER

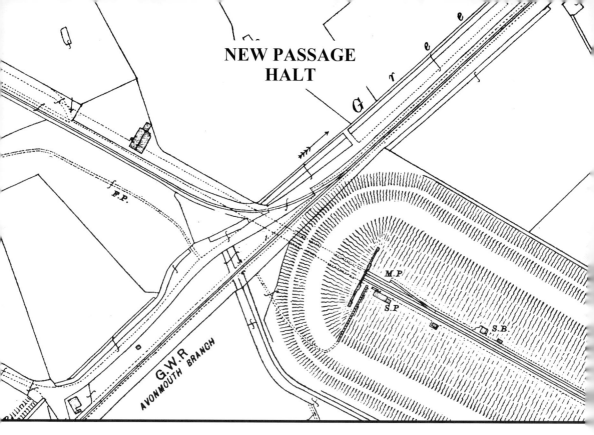

NEW PASSAGE HALT

XVI.   The eastern portal of the Severn Tunnel is right of centre on this 1920 map and the 1900 goods line from Avonmouth to Pilning Junction is from lower left to top right. Curving from it, through a gate, is the siding to Sea Wall Pumping Station. It conveyed coal to the pumps used to help reduce water levels in the Severn Tunnel. These were electrified in 1963 and the traffic ceased. There had been a camp in this vicinity for tunnel construction workers. The huts were wooden with a central hearth and chimney of brick. One of these heavy structures disappeared down into the tunnel workings one night, taking with it the sleeping mens' trousers and waistcoats, these having been hooked onto it to dry.

85.   The halt was opened on 9th July 1928 and was situated beyond the top border of the map, close to Redwick. (See also the top of map XIV.) This view is from 1930. The platform was on the north side of the line and closed on 23rd November 1964. Tickets were issued by an agent from a nearby house. (LGRP/NRM)

NEW PASSAGE PIER

XVII.　　The 1881 edition features the B&SWUR shore station and part of its pier (top left)for the ferry to Portskewett. These were in use from 8th September 1863 to 1st December 1886, when passengers were able to pass under the Severn Estuary. The siding on the left turned south to Sea Wall Pumping Station. It was replaced by the siding shown on the previous map in 1900 and the remainder of the track was lifted in 1917, although long out of use.

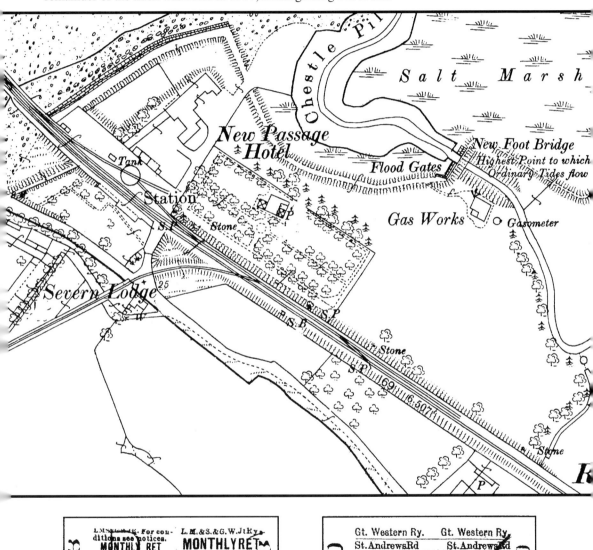

86.   The flags were flying and the marquees were up for the opening day. The hotel is on the left. There were stations at both ends of the massive timber structure and a signal box at each end. One had 16 levers and the other 5. In 1881, there was a station master, a ticket collector and ten porters. There were also 14 men involved with the two steam ferries. (M.Oakley coll.)

87.   The landward part of the pier was still to be seen in April 1973. The first Severn Road Bridge is in the background. (T.J.Edgington)

CROSS HANDS HALT

88.   This halt was less than half a mile from New Passage Halt and was in use between the same dates. Photographed in 1964, it was situated on the south side of the line. The fixed distant signal was for Pilning Low Level. (Stations UK)

89.   Ever optimistic, the GWR built the structures for double track, but economised by providing timber facings on the platform. (Lens of Sutton coll.)

PILNING LOW LEVEL

XVIII.   The 1881 survey appears to show a platform on the north side of the New Passage Pier line. The siding is shown on the south side, but the points have been omitted. "Detached No. 12" refers to a remote fragment of another parish. The line remained in place, but was little used between 1886 and 1900. Coal for the pumping station was the main traffic.

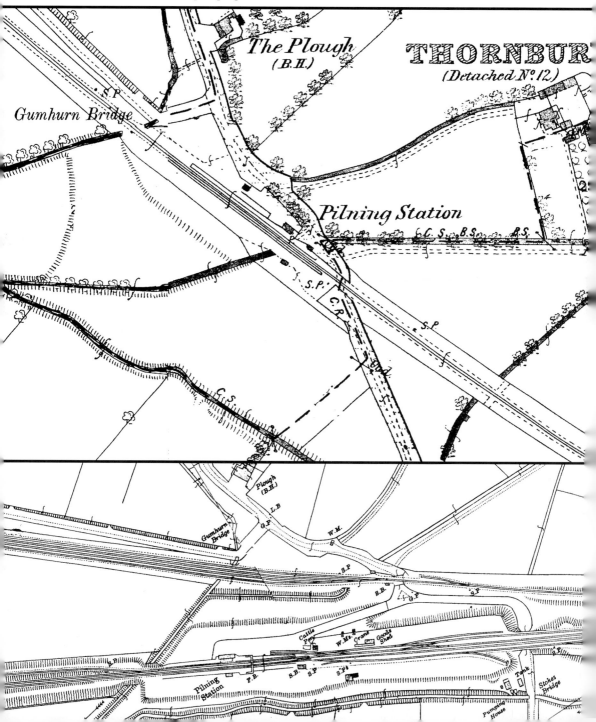

90.	Expense was kept to the minimum in 1928 with most components being of timber. This panorama is from 1959. At the Pilning stations there were on average 27 men throughout the 1930s. (P.J.Garland/R.S.Carpenter)

XIX.	The 1920 survey has been reduced to 17 ins to 1 mile and rotated slightly. The Low Level station was built on the site of the original one in 1928, to the right of Gumhurn Bridge. The parallel sidings near it were for goods traffic to and from the 1900 link with Avonmouth. Lower left is the 1886 station and the main line to the Severn Tunnel.

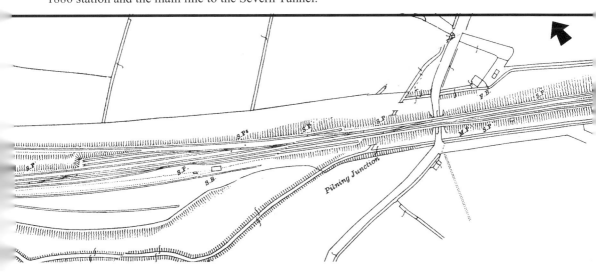

Pilning High Level appears in pictures 66 to 73 in our _Swindon to Newport_ album.

91.   The waiting shelter carried the obligatory fire bucket, which was of particular value in the days of steam when locomotives were prone to ignite sleepers. The goods trains have gone, to be replaced by a few condemned wagons. (Lens of Sutton coll.)

92.   A DMU waits to depart for Severn Beach on 12th March 1960. The signal box was built in 1917 and named "Pilning Branch Box". It was in use until the line closed completely on 1st September 1968. One gate post remained in place in 2004. (M.A.N.Johnston)

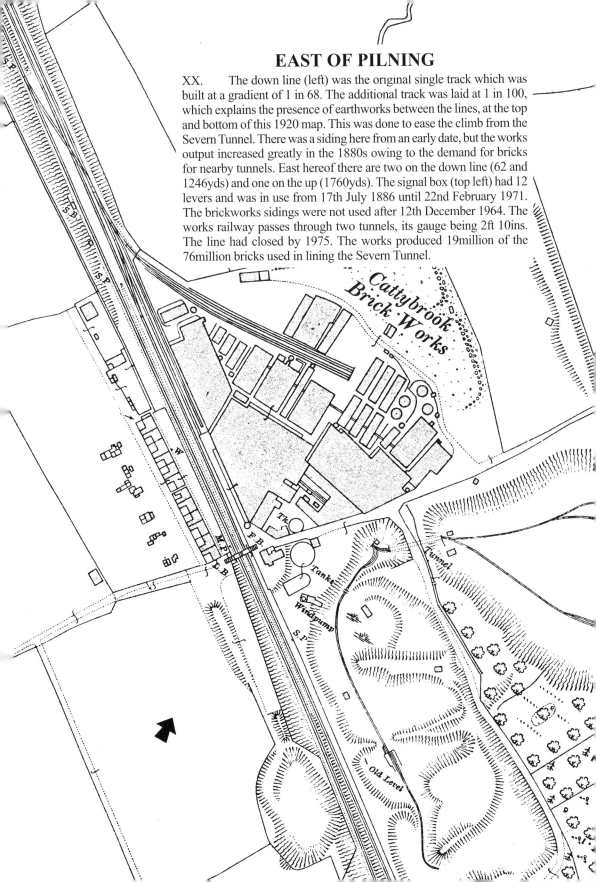

EAST OF PILNING

XX.　　The down line (left) was the original single track which was built at a gradient of 1 in 68. The additional track was laid at 1 in 100, which explains the presence of earthworks between the lines, at the top and bottom of this 1920 map. This was done to ease the climb from the Severn Tunnel. There was a siding here from an early date, but the works output increased greatly in the 1880s owing to the demand for bricks for nearby tunnels. East hereof there are two on the down line (62 and 1246yds) and one on the up (1760yds). The signal box (top left) had 12 levers and was in use from 17th July 1886 until 22nd February 1971. The brickworks sidings were not used after 12th December 1964. The works railway passes through two tunnels, its gauge being 2ft 10ins. The line had closed by 1975. The works produced 19million of the 76million bricks used in lining the Severn Tunnel.

Cattybrook Brick Works

Tunnel

Tk.

F.B.

M.P.

L.B.

Tanks

Windpump

S.P.

Old Level

W

93.   A "Grange" passes the chimney of Cattybrook Brickworks on a special up working in about 1960. A 13-ton mineral wagon can be seen on the sidings serving the brickworks. (D.J.Cross)

PATCHWAY

Patchway Station

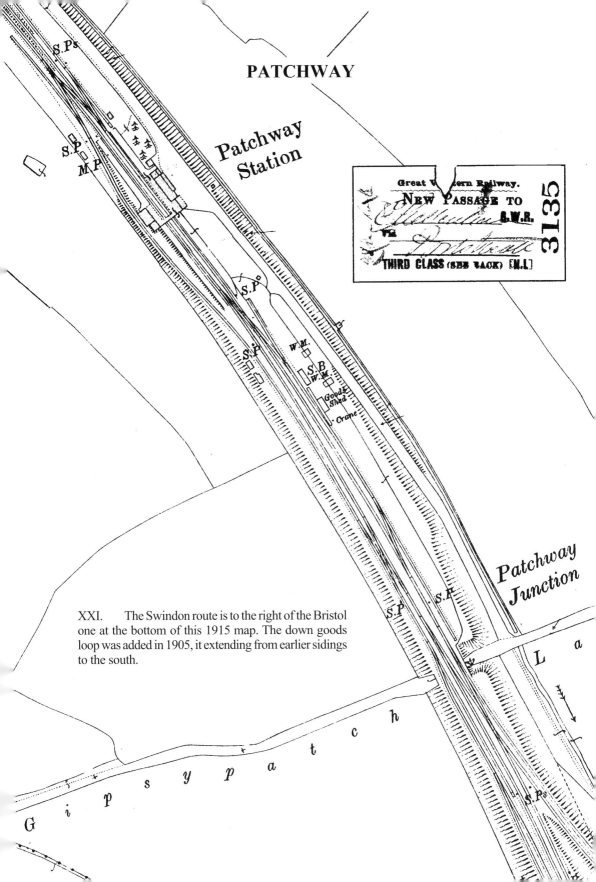

Patchway Junction

XXI.   The Swindon route is to the right of the Bristol one at the bottom of this 1915 map. The down goods loop was added in 1905, it extending from earlier sidings to the south.

94.   The first station was north of the present one, beyond the bridge in the distance. The latter was provided for agricultural purposes. A goods line passes to the left of the station, which opened on 10th August 1885 as "Patchway & Stoke Gifford". The suffix was dropped in 1908. (M.Oakley coll.)

This station appears in *Swindon to Newport* in pictures 57 to 62.

95.   Photographed on 4th June 1960 was class 3 2-6-2T no. 82006 with a down local train. The signal box had a 45-lever frame and functioned between 19th October 1902 and 22nd February 1971. The down loop was not used after 1967 and staffing ceased in 1968. Only a roofless footbridge now remains, but there was a train in most hours on weekdays in 2004. The journey towards Bristol continues at picture 106. (M.Hale/M.Oakley coll.)

3. Chittening Platform to Ashley Hill

CHITTENING PLATFORM

96.   The 1910 line between Avonmouth and Filton Junction served unexpected purposes with the advent of World War I and the construction of a factory. It had five sidings. Belatedly platforms were provided from 13th November 1918 to 11th October 1923. The ones seen were in use from 27th October 1941 until 1st August 1946. They were reopened for workers from 25th August 1947 and to the public on 31st May 1948. Closure took place on 23rd November 1964. No trace remains. (Stations UK)

HALLEN HALT

XXII.   A public service was available from 9th May 1910 to 22nd March 1915. The halt was in use again in 1917-18 for factory workers only. It was half a mile southeast of the village and is shown on the 1915 survey. The track was doubled here in 1917 and a siding was provided on the south side of the line for an Air Ministry fuel depot in June 1940. When closed in July 1973, this siding was used by Texaco.

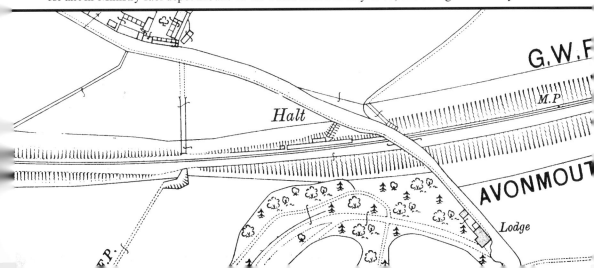

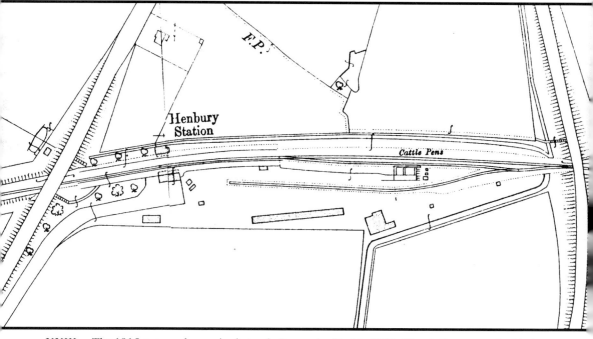

XXIII. The 1915 survey shows single track. It was doubled in 1917. The station opened with the line in 1910.

97. An ex-GWR railcar leaves the station in the mid-1950s on one of the daytime "circular" Temple Meads workings via Clifton Down to Avonmouth and then back via Henbury and Filton Junction. The goods yard was in use until 5th July 1965. (G.A.Nicholls coll.)

98.   The station employed only three men throughout the 1920s and 30s. The building on the left was still standing in 2004, although much overgrown. The photo is from 1955. (Stations UK)

99.   Class 9F 2-10-0 no. 92086 heads an Avonmouth to Bromford Bridge oil train on 21st September 1962. Passenger service ceased on 23rd November 1964 and singling followed on 22nd May 1966. The station is now on the edge of the urban area of Bristol and has a greater traffic potential than Severn Beach. (D.J.Cross)

CHARLTON HALT

100. The halt opened with the line, but closed on 23rd March 1915 with less than five years use. Charlton Tunnel is 302yds in length and passes through the same ridge as the Patchway Tunnels. (BR/M.Oakley coll.)

XXIV. The 1915 survey shows the footpath at a different angle from the one built. The village was destroyed during the extension of the Filton runway for the Brabazon aircraft in 1947.

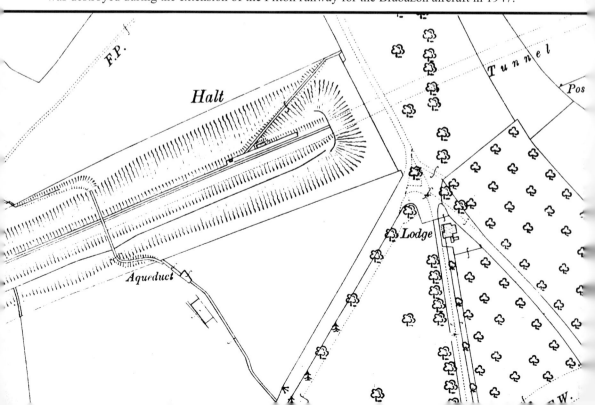

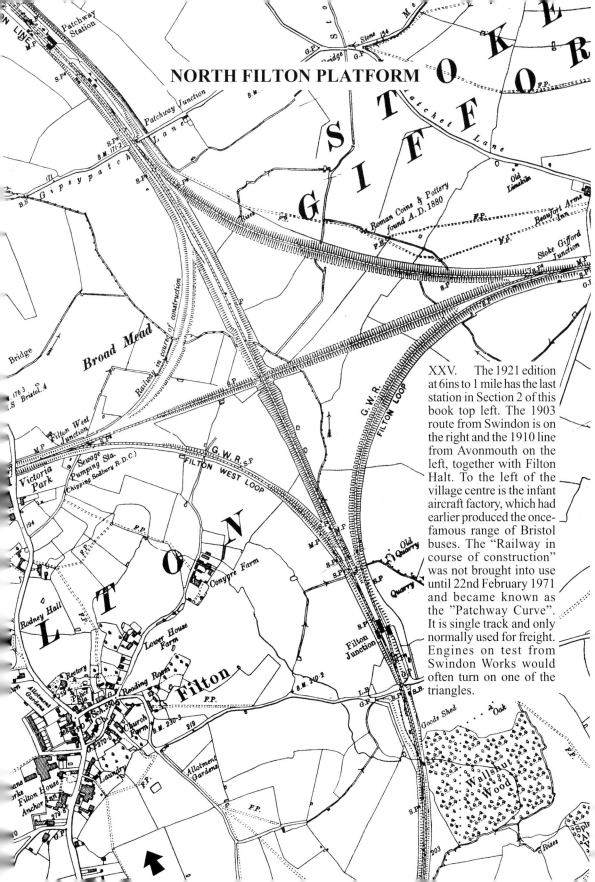

XXV. The 1921 edition at 6ins to 1 mile has the last station in Section 2 of this book top left. The 1903 route from Swindon is on the right and the 1910 line from Avonmouth on the left, together with Filton Halt. To the left of the village centre is the infant aircraft factory, which had earlier produced the once-famous range of Bristol buses. The "Railway in course of construction" was not brought into use until 22nd February 1971 and became known as the "Patchway Curve". It is single track and only normally used for freight. Engines on test from Swindon Works would often turn on one of the triangles.

101.   Filton Halt was in use for less than five years, the dates being as for Charlton Halt. Included are the signals for Filton West Junction. The halt reopened on 12th July 1926 as "North Filton Platform". (BR/M.Oakley coll.)

←⎯⎯⎯⎯

102.   A longer and more substantial platform was built and a second one added. The original Pagoda shelter was supplemented by less elegant ones, together with roofless toilet blocks. The next picture is from the other side of the bridge in the distance; it carries the A38. Doubling of the route to Hallen Marsh Junction took place in stages in 1917, singling followed in 1966 and it was doubled again in 1994, mainly for coal traffic from Avonmouth to Didcot. (LGRP/NRM)

103.   In the distance is the embankment of the 1863 route to New Passage Pier. The bridge in it dates from 1910. Centre is Filton West signal box, which had 30 levers and functioned from the opening of the line until 22nd July 1971. To the left of it are three carriage sidings, which came into use on 27th July 1942 for berthing aircraft workers trains.
(P.J.Garland/G.A.Nicholls coll.)

104. A westward view from the other side of the A38 bridge in 1964 includes a large part of the Bristol Aeroplane Company's works. The massive building erected in 1947 to build the Brabazon airliner (the largest with propellers) was later used for the construction of the Concordes. The bridge links the BAC sites and recently provided access for visitors to the last-built Concorde at its final resting place. On the right are the signals for the junction, plus a shunt signal for the carriage sidings. They are duplicated on the left for trains starting from the down platform. DMUs operated workmens services from it until 12th May 1986. (Stations UK)

105. A 30yd wide level crossing was constructed in 1947 to allow the new larger aircraft to cross the line from the works to the runways. The electrically operated sliding barriers were interlocked with the signals at Filton West box and are seen in 1980. They were in regular use in the next century, controlled from Bristol. The BAC had a siding prior to 1947, south of the line. (C.G.Maggs)

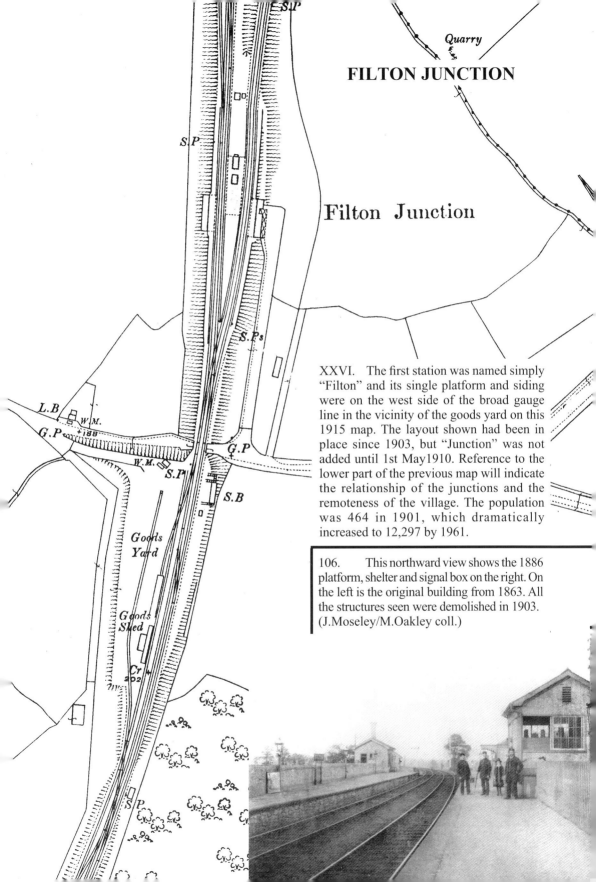

FILTON JUNCTION

Quarry

Filton Junction

XXVI. The first station was named simply "Filton" and its single platform and siding were on the west side of the broad gauge line in the vicinity of the goods yard on this 1915 map. The layout shown had been in place since 1903, but "Junction" was not added until 1st May 1910. Reference to the lower part of the previous map will indicate the relationship of the junctions and the remoteness of the village. The population was 464 in 1901, which dramatically increased to 12,297 by 1961.

106.   This northward view shows the 1886 platform, shelter and signal box on the right. On the left is the original building from 1863. All the structures seen were demolished in 1903. (J.Moseley/M.Oakley coll.)

S.P

S.P

S.Ps

L.B
W.M.
+188
G.P

W.M.
S.P

G.P

S.B

Goods
Yard

Goods
Shed

Cr
202

S.P

BRISTOL, CLIFTON DOWN, AVONMOUTH DOCK and SEVERN BEACH

Miles	Miles		Week Days																				
			am ❸		am	am	am		am	am ❸		am	am		am	am	am	am		am		am ❸	am
—	—	**Bristol** (Tem. Meads) dep	**5 10**	..	..	..	**5 47**	..	**6 0**	**6 2**	..	**6 14**	..	..	**6 35**	**6 45**	**6 50**	**7 0**	..	..	..	**7 22**	**7 30**
1	1	„ (Law. Hill)	5 14	..	5 36	..	5 50	..	6 8	6 7	..	6 17	..	..	6 39	6 50	6 54	7 4	..	7 16	..	7 26	7 35
1½	1½	„ (Stap. Road)	5 17	..	5 40	..	5 54	..	6 15	6 11	..	6 20	..	..	6 42	6 53	6 57	7 7	..	7 19	..	7 29	7 39
—	2½	Ashley Hill	..	..	5 45	..	5 58	..	..	6 16	..	..	..	..	6 46	..	7 1	..	..	..	..	7 33	7 43
—	3¾	Horfield	..	..	..	..	6 2	..	..	6 20	..	6 27	..	..	6 50	..	7 6	..	..	..	..	7 37	7 47
—	4¾	Filton Junction	..	..	5 50	..	6 5	..	..	6 24	..	6 31	..	..	6 54	..	7 10	..	..	..	..	7 40	7 51
—	5¾	North Filton Platform	..	..	..	..	..	..	..	6 26	..	..	..	..	6 57	..	7 14	..	..	..	..	..	..
—	8	Henbury	..	..	..	..	..	..	..	6 31	..	..	..	..	7 2	..	7 19	..	..	..	..	..	..
—	10½	Chittening Platform	..	..	..	..	..	..	..	..	..	..	..	..	7 7	..	7 24	..	..	..	..	..	..
—	12	St. Andrew's Road	..	..	..	..	..	..	..	6 40	..	..	..	..	7 14	..	7 30	..	..	..	..	..	..
2¾	—	Montpelier	5 21	..	..	..	..	..	6 19	..	..	..	..	..	..	6 58	..	7 11	..	7 23	..	..	..
3¼	—	Redland	..	..	..	..	..	..	6 22	..	..	..	..	..	..	7 0	..	7 14	..	7 25	..	..	..
4	—	Clifton Down	5 26	..	..	..	..	..	6§31	..	..	..	..	..	..	7 3	..	7 17	..	7 28	..	..	..
6	—	Sea Mills	5 30	..	..	..	..	..	6 36	..	..	..	..	..	..	7 7	..	7 21	..	7 32	..	..	..
7½	—	Shirehampton	5 34	..	..	..	..	..	6 42	..	..	..	..	..	..	7 11	..	7 25	..	7 36	..	..	..
9	13	**Avonmouth Dock** arr	**5 38**	..	..	..	..	..	**6 46**	**6 43**	..	..	..	..	**7 17**	**7 15**	**7 33**	**7 29**	..	**7 40**	..	..	..
		dep	**5 42**	..	..	**6 10**	..	..	**6 50**	..	..	..	**7 5**	..	..	**7 20**	..	**7 32**	..	..	..	..	..
10	14	St. Andrew's Road	5 46	..	..	6 13	..	..	6 54	..	..	..	7 8	..	..	7 24	..	7 38	..	..	..	..	..
13½	17½	**Severn Beach** arr	..	..	..	**6 21**	..	..	..	..	..	..	**7 16**	..	..	..	..	**7 46**	..	..	..	..	

	Week Days—*continued*																					
	am ❷	am	am	am ❸	am	am		am	am	am ❸	am	am	am		am	am	am	pm	am	noon		pm ❸
Bristol (Tem. Meads) dep	**7 42**	**8 0**	**8 25**	**8 37**	**9 0**	**9 5**	..	**9 10**	**10 0**	**10 50**	**1050**	**11E 0**	**11 9**	..	**11 15**	..	..	..	**1150**	**12 0**	..	**1235**
„ (Law. Hill)	7 46	8 4	8 28	8 41	9 4	..	..	9 16	10 4	10 54	..	11 4	11 14	..	11 19	1122	1135	..	1155	12 4	..	1238
„ (Stap. Road)	7 49	8 7	8 31	8 44	9 10	9 11	..	9 20	10 7	10 57	11 0	11 7	11 18	..	11 23	1126	1138	..	1158	12 7	..	1241
Ashley Hill	..	..	8 35	..	..	..	..	9 24	..	11 1	Saturdays only	..	Except Saturdays	..	Saturdays only	1130	Saturdays only	Saturdays only	12 1	..	..	Saturdays only
Horfield	..	..	8 39	..	..	..	..	9 29	..	11 5		..		..		1134			12 5	..	..	
Filton Junction	..	..	8 44	..	..	..	..	9 33	..	11 9		..		..		1137			12 8	..	..	
North Filton Platform	..	..	..	..	..	..	..	..	..	..		..		..		1144			1211	..	..	
Henbury	..	..	..	..	..	..	..	..	..	..		..		..		1153			1215	..	..	
Chittening Platform	..	..	..	..	..	..	..	..	..	..		..		..		12 3			..	..	..	
St. Andrew's Road	..	..	..	..	..	..	..	..	..	..		..		..		12 8			1230	..	..	
Montpelier	7 53	8 10	..	8 48	9 14	..	..	Saturdays only	1010	Except Saturdays	..	11 10	..	..	..	Saturdays only	1142	..	Except Saturdays	1210	..	1245
Redland	7 55	8 13	..	8 51	9 16	..	..		1013		..	11 13	..	..	..		1144	..		1213	..	1247
Clifton Down	7 58	8 15	..	8 54	9 19	..	..		1015		..	11 15	..	..	..		1147	..		1215	..	1250
Sea Mills	8 2	8 20	..	8 59	9 23	..	..		1020		..	11 20	..	..	..		1151	..		1220	..	1254
Shirehampton	8 6	8 25	..	9 4	9 28	..	..		1025		..	11 25	..	..	..		1155	..		1225	..	1259
Avonmouth Dock arr	**8 10**	**8 30**	..	**9 8**	**9 33**	..	..		**1030**		..	**11 30**	..	..	..	**1213**	**12 0**	..	**1233**	**1230**	..	**1 4**
dep	**8 14**	**8 32**	..	**9 9**	**9 45**	..	..		**1032**		..	**11 32**	..	..	..	..	**1212**	**1222**	..	**1232**	..	**1 6**
St. Andrew's Road	8 17	8 36	..	9 13	9 49	..	..	..	1036		..	11 36	..	..	..	..	1215	1226	..	1236	..	1 9
Severn Beach arr	..	**8 44**	..	**9 20**	..	..	..		**1044**		..	**11 44**	..	..	..	..	**1221**	..	..	**1244**	..	**1 18**

	Week Days—*continued*																						
	pm	pm		pm	pm		pm	pm ❸		pm	pm		pm	pm		pm	pm	pm	pm		pm	pm	pm
Bristol (Tem. Meads) dep	**1 0**	**1E 7**	..	..	**1 22**	..	**1E30**	..	..	..	**2 0**	..	**2 3**	..	..	**2 35**	**2 35**	**2 40**	**3 0**	..	**3 25**	..	**4 0**
„ (Law. Hill)	1 4	1 12	..	1 24	..	..	1 34	..	..	1 44	2 4	..	..	2 13	..	..	2 39	..	3 4	..	3 29	4 4	4 4
„ (Stap. Road)	1 7	1 16	..	1 30	1 32	..	1 37	..	..	1 47	2 7	..	2 12	2 16	..	2 42	2 42	2 48	3 7	..	3 32	4 7	4 7
Ashley Hill	..	1 19	..	1 34	Saturdays only	..	1 40	..	..	Except Saturdays	..	..	Saturdays only	2 18	..	Saturdays only	Except Saturdays	Except Saturdays	..	..	Except Saturdays	Saturdays only	Except Saturdays
Horfield	..	1 23	..	1 39		..	1 44	..	..		..	..		2 22	..				..	..			
Filton Junction	..	1 27	..	1 43		..	1 48	..	..		..	..		2 26	..				..	..			
North Filton Platform	..	..	..	..		..	1 50	..	..		..	..		Saturdays only	..				..	..			
Henbury	..	..	..	..		..	1 55	..	..		..	..			..				..	..			
Chittening Platform	..	..	..	..		..	..	..	..		..	..			..				..	..			
St. Andrew's Road	..	..	..	..		..	2 4	..	..		..	..			..				..	..			
Montpelier	1 10	..	..	..	..	..	..	..	..	1 51	2 10	..	..		..	..	2 46	..	3 10	..	3 35	4 10	4 10
Redland	1 13	..	..	..	..	..	..	..	..	1 53	2 13	..	..		..	..	2 48	..	3 13	..	3 37	4 13	4 13
Clifton Down	1 15	..	..	..	..	..	..	..	..	1 55	2 15	..	..	..	..	..	2 52	..	3 15	..	3 40	4 15	4 15
Sea Mills	1 20	..	..	..	..	..	..	..	..	..	2 20	..	..	..	..	..	2 56	..	3 20	..	3 44	4 20	4 20
Shirehampton	1 25	..	..	..	..	..	..	..	..	..	2 25	..	..	..	..	..	3 0	..	3 25	..	3 49	4 25	4 25
Avonmouth Dock arr	**1 30**	..	..	..	..	..	**2 9**	..	..	..	**2 30**	..	..	..	..	..	**3 4**	..	**3 30**	..	**3 53**	**4 30**	**4 30**
dep	**1 32**	..	..	..	..	..	..	**2 15**	..	..	**2 32**	..	..	..	..	..	**3 6**	..	**3 32**	..	**3 54**	**4 32**	**4 40**
St. Andrew's Road	1 36	..	..	..	..	..	..	2 18	..	..	2 36	..	..	..	..	..	3 9	..	3 36	..	3 57	4 36	4 44
Severn Beach arr	**1 44**		..	..	..	..	..	..	..	..	**2 44**	..	..	..	..	..	**3 17**	..	**3 44**	..	**4 5**	**4 44**	**4 52**

PILNING (Low Level), SEVERN BEACH and AVONMOUTH DOCK

Mile		Week Days																				
		am	am	arn	am	am	am	am	am	am	am	am	am	noon	pm	pm	pm	pm	pm	pm	pm	pm	pm
								S	E⊛	V			E⊛	E	S			S			S	E		E
—	Bristol ⎧ T. Meads dep	..	..	7 30	..	825	..	9 10	..	..	..	1050	..	..	..	..	1K 7	..	2F 0	..	..	..	..
1	⎨ Law. Hill	..	..	7 35	..	828	..	9 16	..	..	..	1054	..	..	..	..	1 12	..	2 13	..	..	..	..
1½	⎩ Stapleton Rd.	..	..	7 39	..	831	..	9 20	..	..	..	1057	..	..	..	..	1 16	..	2 16	..	..	..	..
2¼	Ashley Hill	..	..	7 43	..	835	..	9 24	..	..	..	11 1	..	..	..	..	1 19	..	2 18	..	..	..	..
3½	Horfield	..	..	7 47	..	839	..	9 29	..	..	..	11 5	..	..	..	..	1 23	..	2 22	..	..	..	..
4¾	Filton Junction	..	..	7 51	..	844	..	9 33	..	..	..	11 9	..	..	..	..	1 27	..	2 26	..	..	..	..
6	Patchway	..	..	7 56	..	849	..	9 37	..	..	..	1113	..	..	..	..	1 31	..	2 30	..	..	..	..
9¼	Pilning (High Level) arr	..	..	8 2	..	857	..	..	..	..	..	..	..	..	..	..	..	..	..	..	..	..	..
9½	Pilning (Low Level).. dep	..	..	8 10	..	..	9 45	9 50	..	..	1123	..	..	..	1 40	..	2 38	..	..	..	..		
10¼	Cross Hands Halt	..	..	8 12	..	..	9 47	9 52	..	..	1125	..	..	..	1 42	..	2 40	..	..	..	..		
10¾	New Passage Halt	..	..	8 14	..	..	9 49	9 55	..	..	1127	..	..	..	1 44	..	2 42	..	..	..	..		
11¾	Severn Beach ⎰ arr	..	..	8 17	..	..	9 52	9 57	..	..	1130	..	..	..	1 47	..	2 45	..	..	..	..		
	⎱ dep	6 43	7 35	8 23	9 0	..	..	..	10 0	11 0	..	12 0	1223	1 0	1 25	..	2 0	..	3 0	3 35	4 0	4 20
15¼	St. Andrew's Road	6 51	7 44	8 30	9 8	..	..	10 8	11 8	..	12 8	1230	1 8	1 33	..	2 12	..	3 8	3 43	4 8	4 27	
16¼	Avonmouth Dock.. arr	6 54	7 47	8 34	9 11	..	..	10 11	11 11	..	1213	1233	1 11	1 36	..	2 15	..	3 11	3 46	4 11	4 30	
—	Avonmouth Dock dep	7 20	7 52	..	8 35	..	9 15	..	..	10 15	1115	..	1215	1235	15 1	1 40	..	2 16	..	3 15	3 50	4 15	4 32
17¾	Shirehampton	7 24	7 56	..	8 40	..	9 19	..	..	10 19	1119	..	1219	1239	19 1	1 45	..	2 20	..	3 19	3 54	4 19	4 36
19¼	Sea Mills	7 28	8 1	..	8 45	..	9 23	..	..	10 23	1123	..	1223	1243	23 1	49	..	2 24	..	3 23	3 58	4 23	4 40
21¼	Clifton Down	7 36	8 8	..	8 52	..	9 30	..	..	10 30	1130	..	1230	1250	30 1	1 58	..	2 31	..	3 30	4 5	4 30	4 47
22	Redland	7 38	8 10	..	8 54	..	9 32	..	..	10 32	1132	..	1232	1252	32 2	0	..	2 33	..	3 32	4 7	4 32	4 49
22½	Montpelier	7 40	8 12	..	8 57	..	9 34	..	..	10 34	1134	..	1234	1255	34 2	2	..	2 35	..	3 34	4 9	4 34	4 51
23¾	Bristol ⎧ Stapleton Rd.	7 45	8 16	..	9 1	..	9 38	..	..	10 38	1138	..	1238	1259	38 2	9	..	2 39	..	3 38	4 13	4 38	4 56
24¼	⎨ Law. Hill	7 48	8 19	..	9 3	..	9 41	..	..	10 41	1141	..	1241	2 1	41 2	11	..	2 42	..	3 41	4 16	4 41	5 0
25¼	⎩ T. Meads arr	7 52	8 23	..	9F16	..	9 45	..	..	10E45	1145	..	1245	..	1D45	..	2 46	..	3E45	4 20	4E48	5 5	

D Arr 1 48 pm on Saturdays
E or E̶ Except Saturdays
F Change at Stapleton Road
G On Saturdays dep Bristol (Temple Meads) 5 0 pm and change at Stapleton Road

H Saturdays only; also runs Mondays to Fridays, 25th July to 26th August inclusive
K On Saturdays dep Bristol (Temple Meads) 1 0 pm and change at Stapleton Road
N Third class only

S or S̶ Saturdays only
V Third class only on Mondays to Fridays. First and Third class on Saturdays
Z 8 minutes later Mondays to Fridays
⊛ Third class only

The timetables show morning and afternoon trains in June 1955. There were also three stopping trains from Bristol to Swindon calling at Filton Junction on weekdays.

107.   A 1954 northward panorama from the signal box includes the lines curving left to Filton West Junction and right to Stoke Gifford Junction. The road to the passenger entrance is also on the right. The number of staff at the station increased from 14 in 1913 to 24 in 1938. (Stations UK)

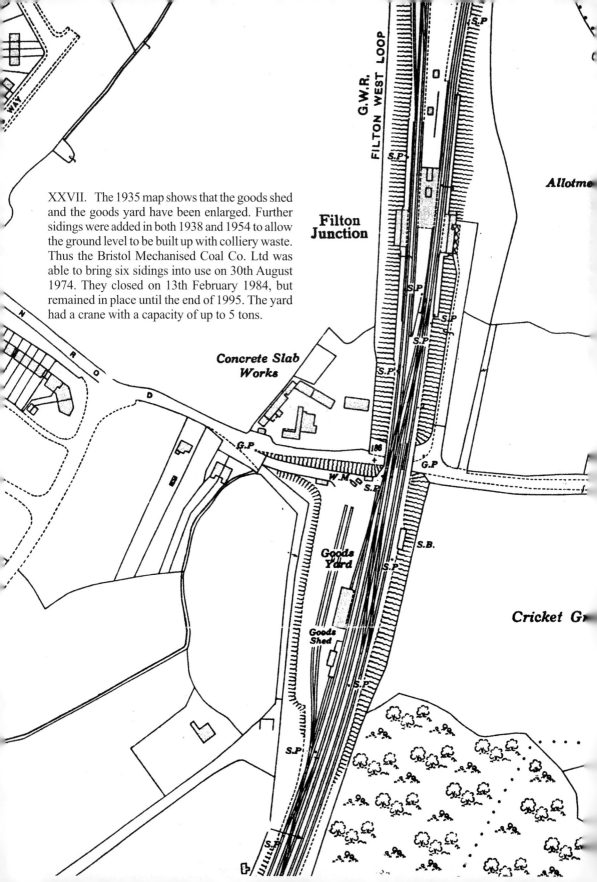

XXVII. The 1935 map shows that the goods shed and the goods yard have been enlarged. Further sidings were added in both 1938 and 1954 to allow the ground level to be built up with colliery waste. Thus the Bristol Mechanised Coal Co. Ltd was able to bring six sidings into use on 30th August 1974. They closed on 13th February 1984, but remained in place until the end of 1995. The yard had a crane with a capacity of up to 5 tons.

G.W.R.
FILTON WEST LOOP

Filton
Junction

Allotme

Concrete Slab
Works

Goods
Yard

S.B.

Goods
Shed

Cricket G

G.P

W.M.

S.P.

108.   Behind the huts in this 1964 southward view is the goods yard. This closed to general traffic on 5th July 1965. The signal box had a 78-lever frame when closed on 21st February 1971. The building and the frame had both been enlarged. The four tracks southwards were reduced to two on 20th February 1984. (P.J.Garland/R.S.Carpenter coll.)

109.   Prospective passengers were faced with a stiff climb from the road. Seen in June 1978, the roof over the steps had just been removed. The eastern pair of platforms were taken out of use on 6th May 1968 and the suffix "Junction" removed. Staffing ceased in the October following. The station closed on 8th March 1996 and was replaced by the one seen in the next picture. (G.A.Nicholls)

FILTON ABBEY WOOD

110.　　The arrival of the first down train was recorded at 06.25 on 11th March 1996. It was the 05.45 from Gloucester. The main reason for creating the station here was to serve the large new Ministry of Defence Procurement Division office complex, visible on the right. (M.Oakley)

111.　　The first up train came in at 07.14, the 06.15 Westbury to Cardiff, worked by no. 150261. Extra trains were put on between here and Westbury, bypassing Temple Meads. Arrival was 08.22 and departure at 16.55, calling at all stations, work days only. Many staff had been transferred from the Bath office, but still lived in the Bath area. (M.Oakley)

112.   A southward view from the footbridge on 4th March 2004 shows work in progress to create a third track for use by trains bound for South Wales. The connection would be under the bridge in the distance and the brick wall would be demolished to make way for an extra platform. (M.J.Stretton)

113.   No. 158855 departs for Cardiff under the new footbridge span on 28th June 2004, the first day of use of platform 3. North of Filton Junction, the single track was doubled and a crossover was incorporated, adding greatly to line capacity. (M.Oakley)

HORFIELD

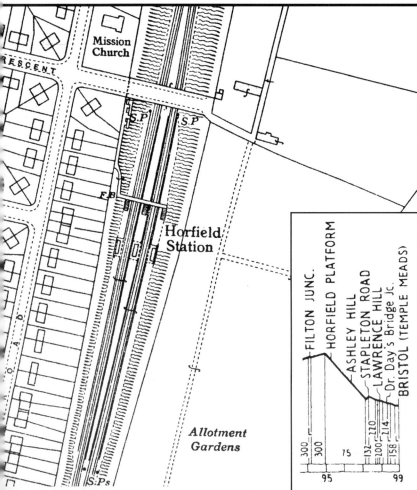

114. Horfield Platform opened on 14th May 1927 to serve a developing area of housing and this 1928 view south records the simple facilities before the quadrupling was completed on 30th April 1933. The suffix was not used after that time. There were no houses on the east side of the line until after World War II. (Brunel University/ Mowat coll.)

XVIII. The 1934 survey shows the revised arrangement and that access was no longer possible from the east side. The 35-lever Filton Incline signal box was in use north of this area until 19th October 1970.

115.   The 1933 rebuilding brought a footbridge with a concrete landing on the approach steps. Note that the original platforms were lengthened at this time. The line drops at 1 in 75 for over two miles into the distance. (LGRP/NRM)

116.   A May 1963 survey includes the road level offices and a banner repeater signal, provided due to poor sight lines of signals beyond the bridge. The station was closed on 23rd November 1964 and little trace now remains, only the platform edges. (M.Hale/M.Oakley)

ASHLEY HILL

XXIX. The station opened later than those on the B&SWUR, on 13th August 1864. The track was doubled in 1886 and is shown on the 1918 survey. The "Boiling Wells" refer to the vigour with which the water emerges. It has caused embankment instability several times.

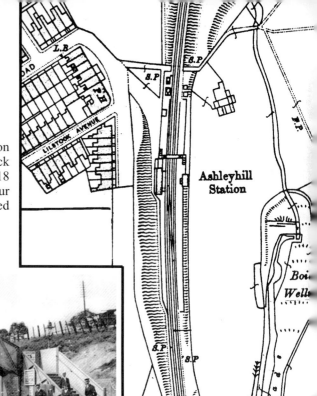

Ashleyhill Station

117. New buildings were erected at the time of doubling. This train is entering the down platform which is on the site of the 1864 original. (LGRP/NRM)

118. An up train fills the platform as passengers arrive with every head covered. Road access was to the left of the main building and, as at Horfield, the residential district was to the west of the line. Throughout the 1930s there were between eight and ten men employed at this station. (LGRP/NRM)

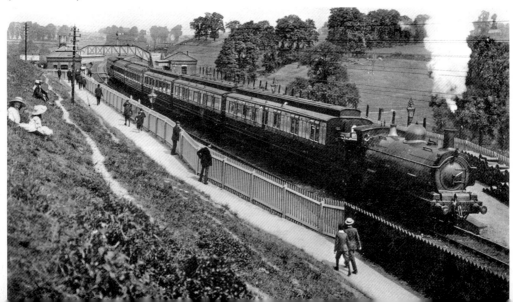

119.   This is the scene after the quadrupling was completed in this area on 30th April 1933. In the distance is the 33-lever signal box, which functioned from 5th July 1925 to 19th October 1970. Behind it was a goods yard of six sidings, which was open from 4th August 1925 to 1st November 1966. (LGRP/NRM)

120.   Local passenger trains ceased to call after 23rd November 1964 and the tracks were reduced to two on 20th February 1984. Electric lighting had appeared by the time that this express graced the station in its declining years. (Lens of Sutton coll.)

Other Middleton Press albums featuring the Bristol area:

Bath Green Park to Bristol
Branch Lines to Clevedon and Portishead
Bristol to Taunton
Bristol's Tramways
Frome to Bristol
Gloucester to Bristol
Swindon to Bristol
Swindon to Newport

MP Middleton Press

Easebourne Lane, Midhurst
West Sussex. GU29 9AZ

A-0 906520 B-1 873793 C-1 901706 D-1 904474

OOP Out of Print - Please check current availability **BROCHURE AVAILABLE SHOWING NEW TITLES**

Tel:01730 813169   www.middletonpress.com   sales@middletonpress.co.uk